THE AWFUL END OF
PRINCE WILLIAM THE SILENT

By the same author

Francis Bacon: Discovery and the Art of Discourse
From Humanism to the Humanities (with Anthony Grafton)
Still Harping on Daughters
Erasmus, Man of Letters
Erasmus: The Education of a Christian Prince
Reading Shakespeare Historically
Worldly Goods
Hostage to Fortune (with Alan Stewart)
Ingenious Pursuits
Global Interests (with Jerry Brotton)
On a Grander Scale: The Outstanding Career of Sir Christopher Wren
The Curious Life of Robert Hooke: The Man who Measured London

THE AWFUL END
OF PRINCE WILLIAM
THE SILENT

The First Assassination of a Head of State
with a Handgun

⟨◆⟩

Lisa Jardine

MAKING HISTORY SERIES
Edited by Amanda Foreman
and Lisa Jardine

HarperCollinsPublishers

HarperCollins*Publishers*
77–85 Fulham Palace Road,
Hammersmith, London w6 8jb
www.harpercollins.co.uk

Published by HarperCollins*Publishers* 2005

1

A catalogue record for this book
is available from the British Library

ISBN 0 00 719257 6

Set in PostScript Linotype Minion with Spectrum
and Castellar display by
Rowland Phototypesetting Ltd, Bury St Edmunds, Suffolk
Printed and bound in Great Britain
by Clays Ltd, St Ives plc

Politics in a work of literature are a pistol-shot
in the middle of a concert, something crude
which it is impossible to ignore.
We are about to speak of very ugly matters.

Stendhal, The Charterhouse of Parma[1]

CONTENTS

List of Illustrations   9
Foreword: The Making History series   11
Acknowledgements   13
Introduction: Accidents of History   15
Map: The Netherlands in the Seventeenth Century   21
Family Tree: The House of Orange   22—23

1 How the Prince of Orange Came to Have a Price
 on his Head   25

2 Murder Most Foul   49

3 A Miraculous Escape   63

4 The Wheel-Lock Pistol – Killing Conveniently   77

5 English Aftermath 1 – 'She is a Chief Mark they
 Shoot at'   99

6 English Aftermath 2 – Pistols and Politics   117

 Finale   135

 APPENDIX 1: A Proclamation and an Edict . . .
 against William of Nassau, Prince of Orange   139

 APPENDIX 2: A copy of the Letters which
 my Lord the Prince of Orange,
 sent unto the Kings and Potentates of Christendom   144

APPENDIX 3: The True Report of the Lamentable
Death, of William of Nassau Prince of Orange . . .
by Balthazar Serack   146

APPENDIX 4: Sir Edmund Neville's Testimony Against
Dr William Parry   152

APPENDIX 5: A Proclamation against the common use
of Dags, Handguns, Arquebuses, Callibers, and Cotes
of Defence   155

Notes   159
Further Reading   167
Index   169

ILLUSTRATIONS

The assassination of the Duke of Guise. *(Author's collection)*   18

William I 'the Silent' of Orange. Engraving by W. Unger after a design by Hendrik Goltzius, 1581. *(Mary Evans Picture Library)*   25

Philip II (1527–98), King of Spain. Engraving by George Vertue (1684–1756) after a portrait by Titian (Tiziano Vecelli, c.1488–1576). *(The Stapleton Collection/The Bridgeman Art Library, London)*   38

The Duke of Anjou's 'joyous entry' into Antwerp in 1582. *(Courtesy Rijksmuseum, Amsterdam)*   43

Hogenburg print of Balthasar Gérard's assassination of William the Silent. *(Author's collection)*   49

Seventeenth-century engraving by Stothard of the death of William the Silent. *(Mary Evans Picture Library)*   54

Hogenburg print of Jean Jauregay's 1582 assassination attempt on William the Silent. *(Author's collection)*   63

The wheel-lock mechanism on a sixteenth-century pistol.   78

Portrait of Robert Devereux (1566–1601), 2nd Earl of Essex, 1599 (engraving), by Thomas Cockson. *(The Stapleton Collection/ The Bridgeman Art Library, London)*   86

Portrait of Captain Thomas Lee, by Marcus Gheeraerts (1594). *(Tate, London 2004)*   87

Robert Dudley, Earl of Leicester. *(From the collection at Parham Park, West Sussex, England)*   89

Double-barrelled wheel-lock pistol of Emperor Charles V (c.1540–45). *(The Metropolitan Museum of Art, Gift of William*

9

H. Riggs, 1913 (14.25.1425) Photograph © 1978 The Metropolitan Museum of Art)   97

Elizabeth I. Engraving by R. White. *(Mary Evans Picture Library)*   103

The fireworks display that marked the Earl of Leicester's entry into The Hague in 1585. *(Strong and van Dorsten,* Leicester's Triumph*)*   129

FOREWORD

When Prince William the Silent was gunned down in the hallway of his Delft residence in 1584, his death rocked the cause of Protestantism in the Low Countries. Without their charismatic leader, the Dutch opponents of the occupying Catholic forces of Philip II of Spain looked likely to be brought permanently under the domination of the Habsburgs.

In the event, the Dutch Protestant cause managed to carry on its opposition to the Habsburgs, and eventually succeeded in establishing an independent Dutch Republic. But the assassination of William of Orange with a small, concealed, self-igniting handgun had lasting repercussions across the face of Europe. William had been a marked man for many years, with a Catholic price on his head. Honour and riches had been publicly promised to anyone who could assassinate him. Yet in spite of elaborate security, a lone assassin armed with a hidden pistol was able to penetrate William's 'ring of steel' and shoot him at point-blank range in his own home. After that, no head of state would ever feel safe again, and regimes across the Continent enacted legislation attempting to ban small hand-guns entirely, or to restrict their use in the vicinity of a prominent political figure or head of state.

The assassination of William the Silent, then, marked the moment when new technology intruded into the lives of public figures, emphasising their perpetual vulnerability to violent assault. The event was one of those milestones in history – a marker, a turning point, an epoch-making incident, a directional laser-beam of light from the past to the future – on which our understanding of the past depends. Lisa Jardine's account highlights the extraordinary way in which events on the ground at key moments in history influence forever what comes after them.

The Awful End of Prince William the Silent is the second title in an exciting series of small books edited by Amanda Foreman and Lisa Jardine – 'Making History' – each of which covers a 'turning point' in history. Each book in the series will take a moment at which an event or events made a lasting impact on the unfolding course of history. Such moments are of dramatically different character: from the unexpected outcome of a battle to a landmark invention; from an accidental decision taken in the heat of the moment to a considered programme intended to change the world. Each volume of 'Making History' will be guaranteed to make the reader sit up and think about Europe's and America's relationship to their past, and the key figures and incidents which moulded and formed its process.

Amanda Foreman
Lisa Jardine

ACKNOWLEDGEMENTS

The inspiration for this book came from conversations with two outstanding young scholars of early modern history. As part of her MA in the History of Design run jointly by the V&A and the RCA, my daughter, Rachel Jardine, selected the Belchamp pistol – on display in the British Galleries at the V&A museum – as her 'design object' for a course essay in 'Decorative Arts and Culture of the Renaissance 1400 to 1650'. That was the first time I had ever thought about the technical and aesthetic beauty of the early modern handgun, or considered its lasting impact on history, and I salute her for her expertise, and for the excitement and energy she conveyed for her topic. Dr Robyn Adams wrote her PhD under my supervision in the School of English and Drama at Queen Mary, University of London, on the Elizabethan intelligencer William Herle ('"Both Diligent and Secret": The Intelligence Letters of William Herle', University of London, 2004). While reading through her meticulous transcripts of almost four hundred letters by Herle preserved in the National Archives, I encountered for the first time Herle's vivid accounts of the two attempts on the life of William the Silent. Rachel and Robyn have both helped me significantly in developing my own ideas on William's assassination, and I thank them both.

My colleagues at the AHRB Centre for Editing Lives and Letters have provided me with the ideal environment in which to think and write about the past on the basis of its surviving archives.

I treasure their intellectual friendship and regard myself as exceptionally privileged to be allowed to lead them. The Principal, Vice Principal for Arts and all at Queen Mary, University of London, have, as ever, sustained and supported my research in every possible way. I owe a special debt of gratitude to Professor Morag Shiach, Head of the School of English and Drama, both as a trusted colleague and a much-loved friend.

My debt to my family is, as ever, beyond measure.

Lisa Jardine
November 2004

INTRODUCTION

Accidents of History

William of Nassau, scion
Of a Dutch and ancient line,
I dedicate undying
Faith to this land of mine.
A prince I am, undaunted,
Of Orange, ever free,
To the king of Spain I've granted
A lifelong loyalty.

(First verse of the Dutch national
anthem, the 'Wilhelmus')[2]

FROM THE SIXTEENTH CENTURY down to the present day, Dutch history is saturated with heroic memories of the house of Orange. The Dutch football team wears an orange strip, while its fans sport the Prince of Orange's colours in everything from scarves to face-paints. The Dutch national anthem celebrates the courage of a 'prince undaunted of Orange', prepared to stand up against the tyranny of the King of Spain and his occupying forces, in verses second only to the French 'Marseillaise' in their patriotic fervour (the Low Countries have suffered many occupations over the centuries).

Beyond the borders of the Netherlands, too, there are orange-coloured memorials to the lasting influence of a succession of princes who headed the Orange dynasty. Every July, Orangemen march in Northern Ireland, decked out in orange to remember and to celebrate the victory of a Protestant king of the house of Orange over a Catholic Stuart.[3] The orange and black insignia of Princeton University in the United States is a reminder that the prince of that foundation was a Dutch one, of the house of Orange-Nassau.[4]

In English-language history books, the only member of the Orange dynasty in the Low Countries to feature prominently is William III (1650–1702), who in 1689 ascended the throne of England with his wife Mary Stuart, replacing his Catholic father-in-law King James II, who had been forced to abdicate following the so-called 'Glorious Revolution' of the previous year. Yet the life and actions on the public stage of William III's great-grandfather, William I of Orange (1533–1584) – known to contemporaries as William the Silent (because of his reluctance to speak his mind) and the man celebrated in the Dutch national anthem for his courage against foreign oppressors – played a prominent part historically in the policies of his royal neighbour Queen Elizabeth I and exerted lasting influence over European affairs of state. The manner of William's assassination in 1584 provoked panic at the English court and alarmed Protestant administrations across Europe. It resulted in the decision to commit English forces on the European mainland against the Spanish Habsburg troops of Philip II in 1585 – an eventuality Queen Elizabeth had avoided with characteristic determination throughout almost twenty years of her reign, and a decision which led directly to the launch of the Spanish Armada against England in 1588.

This is the story of William the Silent's murder. Apart from its seismic effect on the European political scene, it was the first assassination of a European head of state in which the weapon used was the new, technically sophisticated wheel-lock pistol – the first pocket-sized gun capable of being loaded and primed ready for use ahead of time, then concealed about the user's person and produced and fired with one hand, in a single, surprise movement. The murder of William of Orange was the first in a long line of iconic killings of major political figures using hand-guns, stretching down to our own day. These include the assassination of Abraham Lincoln during a visit to the theatre, and of the Archduke Ferdinand at Sarajevo which triggered the First World War. As a violent intervention by one man with a gun, calculated to put paid to a political party or movement and to rock a nation to its foundations, William the Silent's murder anticipated the assassinations of Martin Luther King, J.F. Kennedy and Robert Kennedy in the 1960s. The very metaphor of such an action 'triggering' momentous world events derives from the sudden and irrevocable act of firing a pre-primed gun.[5]

The second half of the sixteenth century saw its fair share of sensational gun crimes. Pistols may have been regarded as new-fangled and unreliable by military strategists, who doubted their tactical reliability as weapons of war and mistrusted the highly manoeuvrable light-horse cavalry pistoleers who used them, but they caught on rapidly with civilians bent on mischief. In February 1563, Francis, Duke of Guise was killed while out hunting, by a pistol-wielding Huguenot on horseback. In 1566 a pistol was held to the belly of Mary, Queen of Scots, while assassins stabbed her secretary Rizzio to death in the adjacent room. It was allegedly the sound of a pistol shot close by that led the French queen mother Catherine de Medici to believe that an assassination attempt against the Catholic faction was under way, and thereby

The assassination of the Duke of Guise

set in action the chain of events leading to the infamous St Bartholomew's Day massacre of French Huguenots in 1572.

Religious sectarian conflict figures prominently as a motive for audacious attempts at pistol assassination of key political figures in the early modern period. The internal rifts caused by the doctrinal antagonisms between Catholics and Protestants led to civil war in France, political fragmentation and violent confrontation in the Low Countries, and corrosive political mistrust in England. A brother might betray a brother, or one neighbour might reveal another's secret religious observance. The new handgun was a weapon perfectly matched to the times – a hidden source of confidence, providing its wearer with a ready defence against attack, or a means of sudden, violent death in the hands of a hitherto undetected enemy.

In a Europe saturated with intelligence-gatherers working on behalf of both Catholic and Protestant causes (and the regimes which supported one or other religious party), almost every court and great household had been infiltrated by somebody covertly retained by a contrary faction to carry out local espionage and collect intelligence. A number of these individuals were double agents, serving whichever party currently had the political upper hand. William the Silent's eventual assassin was believed by William's household to be a loyal Protestant recruited as an agent to spy in the Spanish camp on behalf of the Protestant Dutch. In fact he was a secret agent of Philip II, a devout Catholic, who had insinuated himself into the very heart of the Prince of Orange's entourage. His resolute adherence to the Habsburg and Catholic causes in the Netherlands was only uncovered during his interrogation after the event. Then as now, and all too like the suicide bombers of the twenty-first century, intense commitment to his faith gave the assassin the determination to commit an atrocity in circumstances which made it unlikely that he himself would survive the attempt.

In the sixteenth century the handgun – swift, convenient and efficient – became the weapon selected by the high-born individual bent on taking his own life, too. In 1585 Henry Percy, Earl of Northumberland, committed suicide in the Tower of London with a handgun loaded – like the one that killed William of Orange – with three bullets inserted into a single chamber. Because of the disbelief at the idea that a single pull on the trigger could unleash such a triple carnage, it was widely held that Northumberland's death was murder rather than suicide – the shots that killed him were assumed to have been fired by three separate assassins.

William the Silent's assassination preyed on the minds of European heads of state and haunted the imaginations of those responsible for maintaining their security. It was an emblem of the impossibility of preventing a determined intruder, armed with a deadly concealed weapon, from penetrating the most closely guarded of royal enclaves. With some justification those who sought to protect the Prince of Orange believed that the new weapons of war (guns, explosives, potent poisons) made an eventual successful attempt on his life an inevitability. Balthasar Gérard's attack in 1584 was virtually a copycat version of an earlier unsuccessful attempt on William's life, also employing a concealed wheel-lock pistol, also carried out in the prince's private apartments by a supposedly trusted member of his entourage, two years previously.

The pocket pistol became an emblem for the utter impossibility of keeping the sovereign secure. In a vain attempt to prevent the possibility of death-delivering devices being smuggled into the presence of the queen, the English government enacted a law prohibiting anyone from carrying a concealed handgun or firing one within two miles of a royal palace. And in the atmosphere of hysterical mistrust and anxiety that surrounded Elizabeth's person, as the Spanish threatened to strengthen their hold on the Dutch coastline across the North Sea following Orange's demise, several of the litany of supposed plots uncovered in the years immediately afterwards were claimed to have involved audacious attempts on Elizabeth's life with a pistol.

The Netherlands in the
Seventeenth Century

North Sea

EAST
FRIESLAND
Emden

GRONINGEN

Harlingen
Leeuwarden
FRIESLAND
Groningen
Assen

DRENTHE

BENTHEIM

Hoorn Enkhuizen
Alkmaar
Kampen
Zuider
Zee
Zwolle
Bentheim
OVERIJSSEL
Deventer

Haarlem
Amsterdam

HOLLAND

Amersfoort
Zutphen
Leiden
UTRECHT
GELDERLAND
MÜNSTER
The Hague
Utrecht
Arnhem
Delft
Rhenen
Ijssel
Rotterdam
Wijk
Nijmegen
Emmerich
Brielle
Gorinchem
Cleves
Calcar
Dordrecht
's-Hertogenbosch
CLEVES
Zierikzee
Dortmund

Middelburg
ZEELAND
Breda

Venlo
ARCHBISHOPRIC OF COLOGNE
Düsseldorf
Bruges
Ghent
Antwerp
Scheldt
Meuse
Rhine

FLANDERS
BRABANT
DUCHY OF JÜLICH
Cologne

Brussels
Maastricht
LIMBURG

0   25   50 miles

Aachen
Bonn

The House of Orange

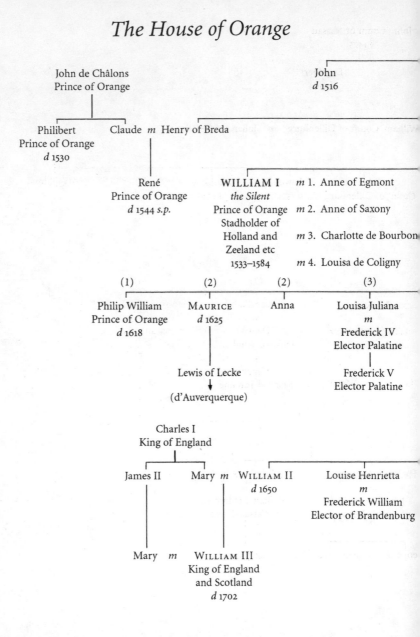

John de Châlons
Prince of Orange

John
d 1516

Philibert
Prince of Orange
d 1530

Claude *m* Henry of Breda

René
Prince of Orange
d 1544 *s.p.*

WILLIAM I
the Silent
Prince of Orange
Stadholder of
Holland and
Zeeland etc
1533–1584

m 1. Anne of Egmont

m 2. Anne of Saxony

m 3. Charlotte de Bourbon

m 4. Louisa de Coligny

(1)

(2)

(2)

(3)

Philip William
Prince of Orange
d 1618

MAURICE
d 1625

Anna

Louisa Juliana
m
Frederick IV
Elector Palatine

Lewis of Lecke
↓
(d'Auverquerque)

Frederick V
Elector Palatine

Charles I
King of England

James II

Mary *m* WILLIAM II
d 1650

Louise Henrietta
m
Frederick William
Elector of Brandenburg

Mary *m* WILLIAM III
King of England
and Scotland
d 1702

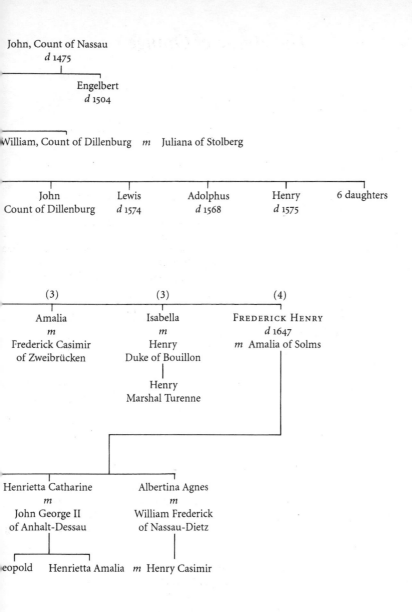

John, Count of Nassau
d 1475

Engelbert
d 1504

William, Count of Dillenburg   *m*   Juliana of Stolberg

| John Count of Dillenburg | Lewis *d* 1574 | Adolphus *d* 1568 | Henry *d* 1575 | 6 daughters |

(3)
Amalia
m
Frederick Casimir
of Zweibrücken

(3)
Isabella
m
Henry
Duke of Bouillon

Henry
Marshal Turenne

(4)
FREDERICK HENRY
d 1647
m Amalia of Solms

Henrietta Catharine
m
John George II
of Anhalt-Dessau

Albertina Agnes
m
William Frederick
of Nassau-Dietz

eopold   Henrietta Amalia   *m*   Henry Casimir

How the Prince of Orange
Came to Have a Price on his Head

BECOMING A DYNASTY

William the Silent, engraving after Hendrik Goltzius (1581)

THE PROTESTANT PRINCE who fell victim to a Catholic assassin's three bullets in July 1584 had not been destined from birth to lead a nation. When William of Nassau was born in the castle of Dillenburg, in Nassau in Germany, in 1533, nobody could have imagined that he would one day become the greatest of all national heroes remembered in the Netherlands – Holland's *pater patriae*', the 'father' of his adopted country, celebrated down to the present day in the rousing stanzas of the Dutch national anthem.[6] The eldest son of William the Rich and Juliana of Stolberg, and a German national, William inherited from his father the comparatively modest title of Count of Nassau. But in 1544 his uncle René of Chalon, hereditary ruler of the small independent principality of Orange in southern France, died on the battlefield, leaving no direct descendants. Orange was a Habsburg possession. After delicate negotiations between the Habsburg Emperor Charles V (of whose extensive empire the Orange territory ultimately formed a part) and William's father, the eleven-year-old William unexpectedly became heir to the Chalon titles. He was immediately removed from his family home and sent to reside at the ancient seat of the Nassau family in Breda in the Low Countries. From there he could be conveniently introduced into Charles V's court at Antwerp, to be raised in a manner befitting the designated ruler of a Habsburg territory.

The suddenness of William's elevation, at such a formative

moment, left its lasting mark. Throughout his life his reputation was as a man of considered actions and a steady temperament – or, according to his enemies, a man who hedged his bets and would never speak his mind. In the public arena he displayed a combination of humanity, seriousness and personal restraint derived from his early modest upbringing, coupled with an easy ability to operate smoothly in the midst of all the magnificence of European court protocol and the procedural intricacies of diplomacy and power politics. His considerable skill as a negotiator depended on a relaxed familiarity with the forms and ceremonies of international power-broking, acquired during his period in the household of Charles V. Over and over again in the course of the 'Dutch Revolt' these were the skills needed to persuade ill-assorted parties to sign up to a political alliance, to retrieve lost ground by negotiation, or to gain time or a vital truce, in the all-too-evenly balanced conflict in which William became caught up – most probably against his better judgement – and which consumed the last twenty years of his life.

If William the Silent was not the kind of candidate we might expect for political leadership in the northern Netherlands, neither was he an obvious choice as the leading European protagonist on behalf of the Protestant cause. Although his family was Protestant, he himself was by no means a settled adherent to any sect of the reformed religion by birth or upbringing. One important outcome of the circumstances of his youth was William's complicated attitude towards the religious disputes of the day. During his father's lifetime, the house of Nassau moved closer to the evangelical Protestant princes in Germany. From puberty, however, amid the magnificence of the Catholic Antwerp court of Charles, where the Prince of Orange entered the Council of State on the succession of Philip of Spain as ruler in the Low

Countries in 1555, and was elected a Knight of the Order of the Golden Fleece by Philip in August 1559, it was assumed that William would uphold the Catholic confession of his Habsburg imperial masters. And indeed during his early tenure he showed no inclination to do otherwise.

When Charles V resigned the sovereignty of the Netherlands in 1555 in favour of his son Philip, the ageing Habsburg emperor gave his farewell address to the great assembly in Brussels leaning on the shoulder of Prince William, thereby proclaiming to the world the trust he placed in the young nobleman. Philip II in his turn appointed William governor general or 'stadholder' of the counties of Holland and Zeeland and the land of Utrecht (and other adjacent territories) in 1559, with the task of looking after Habsburg interests in the northern occupied Low Countries territories, and maintaining Philip's 'rights, highness and lordship' there.

In spite of this careful grooming, William of Orange did not live up to the Habsburgs' hopes for him as a loyal servant and administrator of their imperial rule. Instead, the care that had been taken with his upbringing, and the trust placed in him by Charles V, added emotional intensity to the later confrontations between William and Philip II. Philip considered that William had been privileged to have been succoured and supported by the Habsburgs. When the Prince of Orange subsequently became one of their most prominent and dangerous political opponents, the self-appointed defender of the Protestant faith in the Low Counties which the Habsburgs had pledged themselves to root out as a 'vile heresy', this was, for Philip, a personal betrayal.

The principality of Orange was, and is, of relatively small importance on the international scene. Then as now, its main claim to fame was its magnificent Roman amphitheatre and triumphal arch, which dominated the town. Nevertheless, it was William's tenure of that Orange title which singled him out for leadership in the struggle of the Low Countries against the Habsburgs. The Princes of Orange were sovereign princes, and thus, in theory, William was of comparable rank to Philip II – King of Spain – himself. William always maintained that his status as prince removed from him the obligation to pay allegiance to Philip as ruler of the Netherlands. Contemporary political theory maintained that those subordinate to a reigning prince might not challenge his authority unless his rule amounted to tyranny. An equal prince, on the other hand, might voice concern without threatening the established hierarchy or sovereign entitlement to rule. In this respect William was unique among the Habsburgs' provincial governors in the Netherlands and an obvious choice as spokesperson when it came to freely expressing opposition to the way the policies of the Habsburgs were being implemented by those locally appointed to administer the Low Countries territories.

In spite of his theoretically key political position, William for many years avoided any course of action that might set him on a collision course with Philip II. It was apparently this political reticence that led to William's being dubbed '*le taciturne*' ('the tight-lipped'), in Dutch '*de Zwijger*', which was turned in English into 'the Silent'. The soubriquet suggested an irritating tendency in the prince to hold back from expressing his true opinions and a reluctance to take sides. It turned out to be particularly inappropriate as an enduring nickname for a man renowned in his everyday conduct of affairs in private and in public for his eloquence and loquacity.

Following the early death of William's first wife,[7] his second marriage to Anna of Saxony in 1561 was the first public intimation of his desire to distance himself from the Habsburg cause in the Netherlands, doctrinally and politically. Anna was the daughter of the staunchly Protestant Maurice of Saxony, who had died in battle fighting for the Protestant cause in 1553; her guardians were two of the Habsburgs' most prominent opponents in Germany, Augustus, Elector of Saxony and Philip of Hesse (who had been held prisoner by Charles V for a number of years). As anticipated by both camps (Philip opposed the match), William and Anna's marriage created a political focus for anti-Catholic feeling in the northern Netherlands, which came to a head in the mid-1560s.[8]

The immediate issue which provoked confrontation between Philip II and the nobility in the Netherlands was the reorganisation of the bishoprics in the Low Countries undertaken in 1559, and designed to rationalise the existing system of Church authority. Under the reorganisation, direct responsibility for the Church and (above all) its revenues passed to Philip's appointed regent Margaret of Parma and Antoine Perrenot, a prominent attorney from Franche-Comté and influential adviser to Philip II, who had been conveniently appointed Cardinal (at the request of the Habsburg administration), under the title of Cardinal Granvelle. In 1562 the Dutch nobility formed a league aimed at the overthrow of Granvelle (who had been appointed to the key bishopric of Mechelen), on grounds of his excessive zeal in persecuting Protestant heretics, and his complicity in eroding the nobility's secular power and diverting their Church revenues.

Led by William of Orange, the Dutch nobles refused to attend any meetings of the Council of State until such time as Granvelle should be removed from office, thereby bringing the administration of the Netherlands to a standstill. Faced with what amounted to a boycott by the key local figures in the Low Countries administration, Philip withdrew Granvelle in 1564. The gesture, however, came too late to halt a growing tide of opposition against the strong-arm way in which the Low Countries were being run, particularly insofar as this involved a ruthless repression of all reformed religious observance which went beyond anything imposed in Philip's Spanish territories.

At first William, with typical caution, held back from direct defiance of Spanish rule, and it was a group whose leaders included instead his brother, Count John of Nassau, which delivered a petition on behalf of the Dutch people to the regent, Margaret of Parma, in April 1566. Margaret responded by dispatching William of Orange (as local stadholder) at the head of an armed force to subdue the unrest and re-establish full Catholic observance in Holland and Utrecht. William, however, characteristically negotiated a compromise with the States of Holland at Schoonhoven, under which Calvinists – the radical wing of Protestantism – would be given limited freedom to observe their religion openly. This was a position he would take repeatedly in his negotiations over more than fifteen years with local provinces, and it does suggest that he did not consider the strict imposition of either Catholic or Protestant worship a matter of particular importance, temperamentally preferring a broad toleration (though whether for strategic reasons, or on grounds of his own moderate beliefs, is less clear). In 1566 his expressed opinion was that Catholics and Protestants 'in principle believed in the same truth, even if they expressed this belief in very different ways', and this was a view to which he remained committed, although he was unable to prevent those serving under him from taking more extreme positions with regard to the prohibition of alternative forms of worship.[9]

The Low Countries had had a long-standing and widespread commitment to the beliefs and forms of worship of the Reformed

Church, beginning with Luther's opposition to the established Church in the 1520s. The Dutch Revolt started in earnest in the mid-1560s with a spontaneous wave of anti-Catholic iconoclasm, subsequently encouraged by Calvinist outdoor preachers ('hedge preachers') who urged their congregations to cast down the idolatrous worship of Catholicism. Riots and the ransacking of churches and monasteries rapidly spread across the Netherlands. The uprising was put down with ruthless efficiency by forces sent by Philip from Spain under the Duke of Alva (Alba), who arrived as Philip's commander-in-chief in 1568. Calvinist worship, hitherto a tolerated, alternative set of doctrines and practices to which the local authorities had largely turned a blind eye, was driven underground, and many leading Calvinist clergy and their supporters among the nobility fled the country.

Throughout the period of this first Dutch uprising William the Silent tried to maintain a careful balance between the demands of Spanish Habsburg-imposed rule and the commitments and beliefs of the Low Countries he had been nominated to represent as stadholder. Loyal to the Habsburgs who had raised him, he nevertheless sympathised with the broader inclusiveness of Low Countries religious observance and the aspiration of the Netherlanders to self-governance, free from the imposed regime and its foreign occupying troops. When eventually he came under too much pressure from Philip to submit to his authority and impose direct Spanish rule, he resigned his stadholderships and withdrew to his German Nassau territories.

In 1568, however, William of Orange found himself drawn into the Low Countries conflict. He had hoped that his withdrawal to Germany would be taken as a sign of deliberate neutrality. Instead, as part of a ferocious programme of reprisals against the iconoclastic rebellion, Alva's Spanish forces confiscated William's Dutch properties and his revenues. The Counts of Egmont and Hornes were arrested and summarily executed, along with over a thousand 'rebels'. Both Egmont and Hornes had belonged to the 'League of the Great' which had engineered Granvelle's removal, but unlike William they had not gone abroad as the Spanish grip on the Low Countries tightened. Finally, Alva also seized William's eldest son (also named William) from the university of Leuven (Louvain), where he was studying, and took him as a virtual hostage to Spain. His father never saw him again. In spite of his father's repeated attempts to get him back, he remained in Spain, to be raised as an obedient Catholic servant of the Habsburgs (after William the Silent's death, the Dutch refused to acknowledge him as their next stadholder, and turned instead to his younger brother Maurice). Under these provocations, William crossed into the Low Countries from his base in Germany, at the head of an army subsidised by a number of his German neighbours.

William's volunteer forces were no match for Alva and his Spanish army. In 1568 and again in 1570 his military incursions from his German territories were disastrous (Dutch historians refer to them as 'débâcles'), not least because William could not raise the necessary finance from among his allies outside the Low Countries to pay his troops, and was increasingly hampered in his operations by threats of desertion and mutiny. On both occasions he was driven back by Alva, having only managed to secure a number of towns in Holland and Zeeland – the two north-western provinces which fronted the Netherlands coastline, providing control over sea-traffic in the North Sea (or, as the Dutch called it, the Narrow Sea). William's success in obtaining control of Holland and Zeeland was, however, of enormous importance to England, since his domination of the coastline offered Protestant protection from the Spanish invasion the

English feared constantly throughout this period. The English queen, Elizabeth I, though reluctant to be drawn into direct confrontation with Spain in the Netherlands, nevertheless provided a steady stream of soldiers and indirect financing for William the Silent's Dutch Revolt, in her own interests.

A historical turning point for the Orange cause – though not military success – came in 1572. As so often in the story of the Dutch Revolt, the gains made by William the Silent (who on this occasion also was eventually forced to concede victory and withdraw) derived as much from political events outside the Netherlands as from the outcomes of specific battles and sieges within the provinces themselves.[10] In May 1572 the strategically important town of Mons on the French–Low Countries border went over to the Protestant cause. Mons had been heavily fortified by Charles V as a border stronghold at the time of his wars against France. Its almost impregnable walls were now defended by Count Louis of Nassau and a group of supporters of the Orange cause, with the help of a contingent of French Huguenots (a total of around 1,500 troops) and about a thousand local Protestant supporters. An independent provincial government was set up in the town and Calvinist worship made legal (contravening the explicit prohibitions of Philip II and his Inquisition).

The French king, Charles IX – vacillating between Catholic and Protestant causes in his own civil-war-torn country – was known to be considering an invasion of the Low Countries in support of the Protestant Huguenot cause, with the strategic political objective of confronting Spain in the arena of the Netherlands. Alerted to this, and faced with the possibility of a full-scale invasion across the French border, Alva pulled most of his troops back from the heart of the revolt in the northern provinces of Holland and Zeeland, and massed them in Brabant at Mons, besieging the city.

This was a shrewd move, even though it allowed Holland and Zeeland to consolidate their advantage in the north-west.

In mid-June, just before Alva's blockade of Mons became total, Count Louis sent a messenger out of the city to urge the French Huguenots to carry out their promise and mount a massive invasion of the Netherlands in the name of Charles IX. On the advice of his senior, Huguenot-sympathising military commander Admiral Gaspard de Coligny, the French king acceded to the request. On 12 July Louis' messenger, Jean de Hangest, lord of Genlis, left Paris with a force of around six thousand men. Five days later he marched straight into a Spanish ambush at St Ghislain, six miles south of Mons, and almost his entire force was destroyed either by the enemy troops or by the local peasants, for whom the French were still the traditional enemy.[11]

Charles IX, who considered the rout of troops sent on his express orders towards Mons (and surely betrayed into an ambush by Spanish-sympathising intelligencers in Paris) a political embarrassment, hastily tried to distance himself from Coligny's support of the Orangists. On 12 August he instructed his ambassador in the Netherlands to deny his involvement:

> The papers found upon those captured with Genlis [show] . . . everything done by Genlis to have been committed with my consent . . . Nevertheless, [you will tell the Duke of Alva] these are lies invented to excite his suspicion against me. He must not attach any credence to them . . . You will also tell them what you know about the enemy's affairs from time to time, by way of information, in order to please him and to make him more disposed to believe in your integrity.[12]

To the French Catholic party, led by the Duke of Guise and backed by Charles IX's mother Catherine de Medici, Gaspard de Coligny was directly responsible for the French humiliation at Mons. As the instigator of the continuing attempts to persuade the king to declare war on Spain on behalf of the Huguenots, and to engage with Alva's forces in the Low Countries, he became the focus for the Guise party's violent animosity. In August 1572, King Charles finally gave Coligny royal authorisation to invade the Netherlands. On the morning of 22 August there was a Guise-backed attempted assassination of Coligny, which failed when a musket-shot fired by Maurevel succeeded only in wounding the Admiral in the arm. The St Bartholomew's Day massacre, which began on the night of 23 August, was a consequence of this failed assassination attempt. According to the papal envoy in Paris, reporting to the Vatican: 'If the Admiral had died from the shot, no others would have been killed.'[13] The opening move in the massacre was a second attempt on Coligny's life. Having this time succeeded in stabbing him to death on his sickbed, Catholic supporters of the Guise faction went on to murder an estimated two thousand residents of Paris, including all the leading members of the Huguenot party and a number of notable Protestant intellectuals and public figures. The massacre continued in the French provinces well into October, and put paid once and for all to hopes of a major Huguenot force coming to the aid of the Protestant cause in the Low Countries.

William of Orange invaded the Duchy of Brabant from Germany on 27 August with a troop of twenty thousand men, still expecting to rendezvous with the promised French Huguenot army led by Coligny. News of Coligny's assassination and the ensuing mass slaughter of Huguenots only reached him at Mechelen. It was a 'stunning blow', William wrote to his brother Count John of Nassau, since 'my only hope lay with France'. Had it not been for the massacre, the combined Protestant forces would, William believed, have succeeded in relieving Mons and gaining the psychological upper hand in the conflict: 'we would have had the better of the Duke of Alva and we would have been able to dictate terms to him at our pleasure'. On 24 September, having failed to break Alva's grip on Mons, William told his brother that he had decided to fall back on Holland or Zeeland, 'there to await the Lord's pleasure'. A few weeks later he spoke gloomily of making his '*sépultre*' (grave) in Holland.[14] In fact he consolidated the rebel positions there, creating a reasonably secure base for the Orangist forces; he was right, though, in believing that he never would achieve the union of the north-western and south-eastern provinces in a single, Protestant state under his or any other leadership.

In spite of his own profound pessimism, and although history treats his first three campaigns as failed military operations, this was the moment when William the Silent began to be hailed within the Low Countries as the country's hero and potential saviour. The creation in letters, pamphlets and speeches of a potent and lasting image of William the Silent as a man of heroic integrity, fighting selflessly on behalf of freedom for the Fatherland, was the achievement of a group of distinguished intellectuals who formed part of William's immediate entourage. These included Philips Marnix van St Aldegonde, who acted first as the prince's secretary and later as his trusted confidential emissary, Loyseleur de Villiers, who became his court chaplain and close adviser in 1577, and the Huguenot intellectuals Hubert Languet and Philippe Duplessis-Mornay, who joined the prince's household in Antwerp around 1578.[15]

On 19 July 1572, in the midst of the struggle for Mons in Brabant, a political assembly was convened in Dordrecht of representatives of the north-western States of Holland – Holland, Zeeland and Utrecht, the territories largely secured by William

Philip II, Spanish ruler of the Netherlands,
and scourge of Dutch Protestantism

of Orange as Protestant-supporting rebels against Spanish rule.
William did not attend but was eloquently represented by Marnix.
Marnix was a political theorist of distinction, who would in the
course of a long career author a sequence of important republican-
sympathising treatises on the limits of imposed rule. The speech
he delivered at Dordrecht offered a considered version of the right
of the Dutch people to revolt against tyrannical rule, and may be

taken to mark the birth of the Dutch Republic as a reasoned rejection of Habsburg-imposed authority.

On the prince's behalf Marnix fashioned William's image for posterity as the defender of the right of all individuals to freedom of thought and worship. William vowed to the States of Holland, according to Marnix, 'to protect and preserve the country from foreign tyrants and oppressors'. If the States of Holland would acknowledge him as their stadholder, he would lead the Netherlands out of political servitude, returning to them the historic 'rights and privileges' of the provinces and guaranteeing them freedom of worship – 'the free exercise of religion should be allowed as well to Papists as Protestants, without any molestation or impediment'. As a piece of political propaganda William's Dordrecht address was lastingly effective, and has coloured accounts of William the Silent as the heroic defender of freedom against tyranny ever since.[16]

William's image as a 'Christian soldier', fighting for political freedom and freedom of worship on behalf of his oppressed people, was decisively sharpened by the behaviour of the Duke of Alva and his troops once Mons surrendered in mid-September 1572. As the revolt in Brabant crumbled, Mechelen, which had supported William, yielded to Alva without a struggle. To encourage the capitulation of other Orange-supporting towns, Alva nevertheless allowed his men to sack the city. On 14 November he did the same at Zutphen, where hundreds of the town's population were massacred. Finally, on 2 December 1572 at Naarden, as Alva became impatient to engineer a general capitulation in the region before winter set in, he ordered the killing of every man, woman and child in the town.

As one historian of the period has written, 'The slaughter at Naarden, in which almost the entire population perished, only a handful escaping in the dark across the snow, had a sensational effect on the popular imagination in the Low Countries, becoming a byword for atrocity and cruelty.'[17] The ruthless and dogmatic way in which Alva imposed Spanish rule and the Catholic faith on the Dutch people clearly ran counter to any idea of consensual rule – government with the consent and in the interests of the country's population.

REPUDIATING SPANISH RULE

Had Philip II decided to commit the entire massive might of the Spanish military machine to warfare in the Low Countries there is little doubt that the Dutch Revolt could have been crushed. But the Spanish king had other, equally pressing problems to deal with, and there were strong competing claims on his military forces and financial resources. Under the combined burden of paying for the war against the rebels in the Low Countries and that against the formidable navy of the Turkish Ottomans in the eastern Mediterranean, he found it increasingly difficult to raise the necessary credit from bankers outside Spain to pay his forces. In 1573 he recalled Alva from the Low Countries, replacing him with a new governor general who was encouraged to negotiate a peaceful settlement. The terms insisted upon by the rebels, with Prince William's encouragement, however, included a commitment to limited monarchy, with the States General and provincial assembles sharing in government, and a clear statement of the right to free worship. Neither was acceptable to Spain, and hopes of peace evaporated.

Philip could now neither fund his Dutch operations nor disband his troops without payment. In the autumn of 1575 he ceased to be able to finance his mounting debt to his bankers in Genoa and was forced to suspend interest payments – effectively declaring bankruptcy. Royal finances in the Netherlands were completely paralysed. Philip's governor general wrote from the Low Countries:

> I cannot find a single penny. Nor can I see how the King could send money here, even if he had it in abundance. Short of a miracle, all this military machine will fall into ruins.[18]

In November a large, mutinous troop of Spanish soldiers – idle, unfed and unpaid – ran out of control and attacked Antwerp. Orange and his propaganda machine exploited to the full the revulsion felt at the slaughter, pillage and rape that followed in Europe's greatest commercial and financial centre. The 'Spanish Fury' – a major and long-remembered atrocity – confirmed Philip II's rule as that of a tyrant, legitimising armed uprising against him by many who might otherwise have remained obedient to him as their divinely-sanctioned sovereign.

Only for a brief period after Alva's arrival in the Low Countries in 1568, when he succeeded in raising significant but deeply unpopular taxes from the Dutch to finance Spain's military operations, did Philip have adequate resources for military success in one of his theatres of war. In 1571, thanks to Alva's Dutch taxation, the King of Spain was able to send a massive fleet to the eastern Mediterranean and inflict a crushing defeat on the Ottoman navy at the Battle of Lepanto. Even so, the Turks made good their naval losses remarkably swiftly, forcing Philip to allocate an even larger share of his resources to the Mediterranean campaign in 1572, and requiring him to pressure Alva to raise even more revenues through taxation for his Dutch campaign, thereby making the

Spanish regime yet more unpopular in the Netherlands.[19] The arrival of the accomplished military commander Alexander Farnese, Duke of Parma, as Philip's latest governor general in the Low Countries in 1579 brought an escalation in the scale of warfare and increased misery to ordinary Dutch people, but not the looked-for final victory for Spain. As Parma systematically regained control of key towns like Maastricht in the south, the northern provinces consolidated their alliance, and reaffirmed their commitment to William the Silent.

Yet in spite of strong support in Holland and Zeeland, and significant opposition to Spanish rule in Brabant, and although both groups looked to the prince for leadership against Philip II, William could not achieve lasting union between the two. In 1577 he moved his headquarters to Antwerp, where he cultivated local administrators assiduously in an effort to consolidate the Brabanters' resistance, but failed nevertheless to broker an accord between the separate rebellions to collaborate in bringing Spanish rule in the Netherlands to an end. By 1580 a war-weary Prince William, who had by now exhausted most of his personal and family fortunes on financing the revolt, had become convinced that only by inviting in a foreign ruler acceptable to the people of the Low Countries could a stable solution to the conflict be engineered.

William now urged both rebel groups to offer sovereignty over the Netherlands to the Duke of Anjou, younger brother of the French King Henry III, who (having earlier dithered and procrastinated over his involvement) at last agreed to become titular ruler of the Low Countries. In January 1581 Anjou's treaty of acceptance, in which he agreed on oath to abide by the privileges stipulated by the people of the Low Countries, was made public, and in return he was proclaimed 'prince and lord of the Netherlands'. Six months later William succeeded in getting consensus among a significant number of provinces (loosely united under the title of the States General) on a treaty repudiating Philip II and his Spanish heirs in perpetuity, the so-called 'Act of Abjuration'.

It was not, however, until February 1582 that Anjou arrived in the Netherlands. William played a leading role in the warm reception given to him. He was the first to honour the new ruler by kneeling before him as the duke stepped on to the quayside at Flushing on 10 February. William was also prominent when Anjou was installed as Duke of Brabant at Antwerp nine days later. After the duke had sworn the required oath, William laid the crimson mantle on his shoulders, saying as he fastened it: 'My Lord, this

The Duke of Anjou's 'joyous entry' into Antwerp in 1582

mantle must be well fastened so that no one can tear it off Your Highness.' Anjou then rode through the richly decorated streets with Orange at his left hand. Along the route, triumphal arches and processional floats had been set up, representing the role it was hoped Anjou would play as defender of the country against tyranny and restorer of its peace and prosperity. At William's insistence no expense had been spared in celebrating Anjou's 'joyous entry'.[20]

To William's profound disappointment, Anjou's arrival did little to help build a more effective opposition to the Spanish forces, but instead widened the rift between Catholics and Protestants. Anjou's own Catholicism and his insistence on public Catholic worship added to the widespread mistrust of his intentions, as did the fact that the duke had not after all brought with him the large army and financial aid that had been expected. On 18 March an unsuccessful attempt on William of Orange's life was followed by violent reprisals against Anjou's followers, who were believed to have conspired to kill the prince.

Undeterred, William, once he was on the road to recovery, pressed yet harder for consolidation of Anjou's hold over Low Countries government. Anjou's official installation went ahead on the Prince of Orange's own insistence. If the purpose of the 1582 assassination attempt was to prevent the Franco–Dutch alliance, it failed, just as it had, remarkably, failed to end William's life. It is hard at this point to see why William continued to press for Anjou's settled sovereignty. According to his brother, Count John of Nassau, William believed that he could thereby engineer political confrontation between France and Spain, diverting Spanish forces and perhaps Parma from making continued gains in the Low Countries. But however strategically desirable, William's dogged defence of Anjou was increasingly unpopular.

Meanwhile Anjou's own frustration intensified as he awaited the required formal consent of the Dutch people. Finally, he took matters into his own hands. When military reinforcements arrived in January 1583 under their French commander he decided to take effective power over Brabant and Flanders by means of a military coup. Although William was warned by Duplessis-Mornay that Anjou was making treacherous plans to subvert his careful arrangements for the assumption of power, he chose to ignore him. Anjou entered Antwerp at the head of his troops, to the cry 'Ville gagnée, vive la messe, tue, tue' ('The town is taken, long live the Mass, kill, kill'). He expected that his show of force would allow him to take the town without resistance. To his consternation, armed citizens blocked his way, and more than a thousand French troops, including many prominent noblemen, were killed as they fled; around a hundred citizens of Antwerp also lost their lives. After this 'French Fury' – which in its calculating callousness matched anything perpetrated by Alva or Parma in the name of Spanish rule – Anjou's presence in the Netherlands was as much loathed and mistrusted as Philip's had been.

Orange took no part in the defence of Antwerp, and was indeed implicated in Anjou's attack. His fourth marriage, to Louise de Coligny on 12 April 1583, added to his growing unpopularity. Although she was the daughter of the great Huguenot commander assassinated at the outset of the St Bartholomew's Day massacre, she was French by birth, and the union seemed to confirm William's blind determination to forge lasting alliances between France and the Low Countries. In late July 1583, under mounting pressure, William withdrew to Holland, and took up residence in Delft. As confidence in his policy of support for Anjou seeped away, the prince's loyal propagandists Marnix and Duplessis-Mornay quietly resigned and returned to their homes (Languet had died some years earlier). Anjou, chastened and dispirited by the fiasco of his second Antwerp entry, had meanwhile returned to France, leaving his French General Biron in charge of his troops. In June 1584, with negotiations still dragging on to determine the exact nature of Anjou's sovereignty in the Low Countries, word came that he had died.

With no alternative candidate in sight, William was now persuaded to revive negotiations with the northern provinces for his own nomination to the title 'Count of Holland and Zeeland' – an idea first proposed in 1581, and which would have regularised his now anomalous position as unappointed stadholder. Negotiations over the fine print of such an arrangement were still in progress when, on 10 July 1584, William the Silent was shot and killed by an assassin in his Delft home.

WANTED DEAD OR ALIVE

A striking feature of William the Silent's leadership of the Dutch Revolt is the significant part pamphlet publications by both sides played in the unfolding of events. A steady stream of passionate pleas on behalf of each party's cause issued from European printing houses and circulated throughout Europe. Copies of a number of these survive in three or more languages (generally Dutch, French and English), thereby guaranteeing the broadest possible dissemination of the views expressed.

It is against this background of a propaganda war in which – unlike the war on the ground – the Protestant cause was winning hands down, that in 1580 Philip II issued a proclamation inciting all good Catholics and all those loyal to the sovereignty of Spain to seek an occasion to kill William the Silent, and offering the successful assassin a reward of twenty-five thousand gold crowns, together with lands and titles. Like *fatwahs* before and since, the proclamation, which circulated widely in numerous European languages, was strategically counter-productive. The immediate response was the publication of William's 'Apology' – a compellingly-written treatise in which the political theories of Marnix, Duplessis-Mornay and Languet fleshed out into respectability an open declaration of defiance of Spain and Spanish-imposed rule.

There is no doubt that William the Silent was the winner in this pamphlet war. Indeed, such has been the success of the picture painted by him, speaking in the first person (ghosted, probably, by Marnix, Villiers, Languet and Duplessis-Mornay), or by others speaking on his behalf, that it is hard to remember that at the time of his death William did not appear to all those around him as the irenic, tolerant and eminently reasonable man of the pamphlet characterisations. Nor did the Protestant cause he championed, and in which he remained resolutely supported by Queen Elizabeth I of England and her key ministers, Leicester and Walsingham, look as bright a prospect as it had in the 1570s.

On the contrary, by the time of William's assassination many of those around him appear to have been ready to settle for peace at any price. For the first time pamphlets began to appear in which even convinced Protestants urged a reconciliation with Philip II. William himself wrote privately to the unwaveringly supportive Walsingham in January 1584 admitting that in spite of his bravado in public, his country was in a dreadful state:

> I can assure you that the body of this state is much more gravely sick than appears on the outside, and that the evil has gone so far that the most vital organs have long ceased to function. I ask you to excuse me for so often behaving

like the sick, who are ashamed to tell others of their com-
plaints and even try to conceal them as far as they can from
their doctors.[21]

By 1584, not only Philip II, but almost any of the other groups
locked in struggle in the Low Countries could have conspired to
have William the Silent dead, to end the political deadlock. A
proposal to nominate him Count of Holland and Zeeland while
Anjou was alive would have made him a barrier between the
northern rebels and the new ruler, whom they did not trust to
rule them as they wished. Even without that title, William's position was anomalous, since after Anjou's nomination as Lord he
remained stadholder of the two provinces, but had not actually
been appointed (or had his appointment ratified) by Anjou. After
Anjou's death his position continued to be constitutionally awk-
ward. He was recognised and accepted as the States of Holland's
provincial ruler, but without appointment as such, and they continued to grant him political leadership or 'high authority'. Following the Act of Abjuration, William was designated 'sovereign
and supreme head' in Philip's place, but 'sovereign' was carefully
glossed as 'having the High Authority and Government' of the
state.[22] Like Yassar Arafat, William the Silent – once the beloved
figurehead of the revolt or *intifada* – had become, by his anomalous political position, in the end a liability.

2

Murder Most Foul

AT POINT-BLANK RANGE

Hogenburg print of Gérard's assassination of
William the Silent

JUST BEFORE TWO in the afternoon on 10 July 1584,[23] William of Orange rose from dining with his immediate family in his Delft residence, the Prinsenhof, and prepared to withdraw to his private chambers upstairs. Leaving the table and crossing the hallway, he paused briefly to exchange pleasantries with three of the military men protecting him – an Italian officer named Carinson, and two English soldiers who had volunteered to fight for the Orange cause, Colonel Thomas Morgan and Captain Roger Williams. The prince took the Italian by the hand in a gesture of welcome; Roger Williams dropped to one knee, and the prince laid his hand briefly on his head.

As William turned and made to ascend the stairs, Balthasar Gérard, an agent recently recruited to provide intelligence on the activities of the enemy Spanish troops under the command of the Prince of Parma, stepped forward from the assembled company. Pointing a pistol at William's chest, he fired at point-blank range. He had loaded his single-barrel handgun with three bullets. Two passed through his victim's body and struck the staircase wall; the third lodged in William's body 'beneath his breast'. The prince collapsed, mortally wounded. He was carried to a couch in one of the adjoining rooms, where his sister and his distraught wife tried to staunch the wounds, to no avail. William the Silent died a few minutes later.

In the ensuing pandemonium, the assassin dropped his weapon

and fled, pursued by Roger Williams and others from among the party of diners. Gérard was apprehended before he could escape over the ramparts behind the royal lodgings. Cross-questioned on the spot (and, one imagines, brutally manhandled in the process), he 'very obstinately answered, that he had done that thing, which he would willingly do if it were to do again'. Asked who had put him up to the attack, he would say only that he had done it for his king (the Spanish king, Philip II) and his country; 'more confession at that time they could not get of him'. Questioned again under duress later that night he told them that he had committed the murder at the express behest of the Prince of Parma and other Catholic princes, and that he expected to receive the reward of twenty-five thousand crowns widely advertised in Philip II's denunciation of Orange as a traitor to Spain and a vile heretic.[24]

Subjected to extreme torture, Gérard steadfastly insisted that he had acted alone, refusing to name any co-conspirators or to implicate anybody else to whom he might have spoken in advance of his intended action. This act of assassination was, it appeared, the deed of a solitary fanatic, a loner with an intense commitment to the Catholic Church and a faithful upholder of the legitimacy of the rule of Philip II in the Netherlands, and so it was reported in the many broadsheets and pamphlets which circulated the news rapidly across Europe.

The accounts of the prince's death rushed out in the hours following his assassination all stressed the deadly effectiveness of the assassin's bullets by reporting that the victim had succumbed without uttering a single word. Five days after the event, England's head of information-gathering, Sir Francis Walsingham, reported, on the basis of the intelligence gathered from his agents in the Low Countries:

> On Tuesday in the afternoon, as [the Prince of Orange] was
> risen from dinner and went from the eating place to his
> chamber, even entering out of a door to go up the stairs,
> the Bourgonian that had brought him news of Monsieur
> [the Duke of Anjou] his death, making show as if he had
> some letter to impart and to talk with his Excellency, with
> a pistol shot him under the breast, whereof he fell down
> dead in the place and never spake word, to the wonderful
> grief of all there present.

Given the appalling blow the assassination dealt to Protestant
fortunes in the Low Countries, however, more lurid versions of
the stricken prince's dying moments rapidly emerged. 'Last words'
began to circulate, in which, with his dying breath, William
lamented the disastrous impact his death would have on the
United Provinces. The first English printed account of the murder
stated that 'the Prince fell down suddenly, crying out, saying Lord
have mercy upon me, and remember thy little flock'. The Queen
of England herself, sending her condolences to William's widow
ten days after the event, referred to similar sentiments she had
been informed had come from the lips of the dying prince,

> who by his last words, recommending himself to God with
> the poor afflicted people of those countries, manifested to
> the world his Christian determination to carry on the cause
> which he had embraced.

Protestants across Europe needed a narrative of calamitous up-
heaval, the world turned upside down, violent alteration and
lasting damage to the cause. This iniquitous Catholic blow struck
at the very heart of the prince's 'flock' of feuding and disorganised
northern Low Countries provinces; his 'deathbed utterances'
acknowledged the impact his death was bound to have on the
temporary and fragile accord William had managed to impose.

Similarly, early accounts rushed out in broadsheets and pamphlets insisted that the assassin, when seized, refused to speak, while others maintained that he cried out in cowardly fashion, *'Sauve moi la vie, je conterai tout'* (Spare me and I will tell all), and others again claimed that he expostulated: 'What is the matter, have you never seen a man killed before now? It is I who have done the deed and would do it if it were still to do again.' 'And they making him believe that the Prince was not dead, he regretted that more than the punishment which he should receive, and thus was led to prison.'[25]

Like tabloid newspapers' reaction to a politically significant murder today, the sixteenth-century 'press' versions of the assassination and its consequences relished every ghastly detail and, where detail was lacking, invented it to increase the sensationalism of their accounts. Gérard's bullets had cut down the one man capable of sustaining the fragile alliance among the Protestant provinces, each with its separate character and interests, opposed to Philip II in the Low Countries. Without him that accord crumbled and the Spanish regained a firm foothold in the territory. The idea that so drastic an act had been carried out by a stolid, unprepossessing nobody, and that its success had been in large measure the result of a grotesque bungling of the security around the Prince of Orange, was too awful to contemplate. No wonder sixteenth-century chroniclers and pamphleteers felt the need to put brashly unrepentant words in the assassin's mouth.

WHO WAS THE ASSASSIN?

A seventeenth-century engraving of the assassination of
the Prince of Orange by Balthasar Gérard

The cold-blooded killing of the Prince of Orange was high drama
in the volatile political arena of the Low Countries. Its perpetrator,
though, was unnervingly ordinary. Twenty-five-year-old Balthasar
Gérard came from Vuillafans, in Franche-Comté, near Besançon
in France (where you can still visit his family home in rue Gérard
today).[26] Small, quiet and unassuming, Balthasar was one of eleven

children from a well-to-do, devoutly Catholic family, who were also staunch supporters of the Habsburgs as their rulers and benefactors (Franche-Comté had benefited materially from financial investment – and significant tax relief – through its special association with the Habsburgs). He had studied at the nearby Catholic University of Dôle, and it was apparently there that he became determined to fulfil Philip II's request for a volunteer assassin to infiltrate the Orange court and rid him of his prime political adversary. Among the many conspiracy theories which inevitably followed the murder of the Prince of Orange, Gérard's place of origin was judged significant. Antoine Perrenot, Cardinal Granvelle, Archbishop of Mechelen and Primate of the Catholic Low Countries – a figure loathed, feared and eventually unseated by the Orangists – also came from Franche-Comté, and it was suggested that Gérard's family had owed particular allegiance to him.

It does seem unlikely that Gérard had acted without accomplices, or at least without some outside help. He used an elaborate sequence of ruses to gain access to William of Orange's entourage, including forged testimonials and counterfeit sealed documents. Adopting the assumed name François Guyon, Gérard claimed to be the son of an obscure Protestant serving-man, Guy of Besançon, who had suffered persecution for his religious beliefs. To corroborate his story he produced letters signed by prominent figures within the Catholic administration in the Low Countries, which suggested that he was trusted enough by the Spanish to allow him access to classified Catholic information which might significantly help the Orange faction. His documentation had been sufficiently convincing for Pierre Loyseleur de Villiers, William of Orange's close personal adviser, chaplain and intelligence-gatherer, to take him into his personal service on the strength of it, as a messenger and potentially valuable spy. Although in the aftermath of William's death Villiers was briefly arrested and accused of double-crossing the Orange cause, there seems little doubt that he had been genuinely taken in by Gérard's forged testimonials, and particularly by the quality of the sensitive intelligence he had provided by way of introduction.[27]

For several months Gérard came and went between Villiers and William's household, running errands and carrying messages. He did not yet have the necessary level of security clearance to allow him to enter the inner circles around William. However, on 12 June 1584 an extraordinary stroke of luck fortuitously gave him the access and opportunity he was waiting for. As he rode to deliver a confidential message from Villiers to the Duke of Anjou, he was met on the road by messengers bringing news that Anjou had died two days earlier. Gérard seized the moment, and volunteered to ride post-haste to William at Delft to inform him of the death of his close, politically controversial ally. He was admitted into the presence of William himself (subsequently it was said that he was allowed into the prince's own bedchamber because of the urgency of the message he carried), delivered his unwelcome news in a manner that pleased William, and was thereafter accepted by the prince into his intimate circle of followers. Given the assiduousness with which Gérard's credentials were being examined and re-examined before this chance encounter, it must have seemed to him that God had indeed intervened on his behalf.

Gérard now bided his time, waiting for a suitable occasion on which to act. Improvisation seems to have been a key part of the success of his plan. He acquired his weapon (either a single pistol, or a pair) on the very day of the assassination. Seeing a small pistol (or 'dag' as they were commonly called in English) in the hands of one of the prince's immediate servants, he asked if the man was prepared to sell it to him. He had, he told him, shortly to go on a journey, and a pocket pistol would be the ideal weapon to carry to protect himself en route. He may even have been telling the truth – the money used to buy the gun may have been given to him by Villiers to purchase shoes and clothing for the next mission he was to be sent on. According to the broadsheet accounts, Gérard paid a sum equivalent to ten English shillings for the pistol.

In this, as in all other aspects of the planning of the killing, the would-be assassin showed unerring good sense. Gérard could not possibly have entered the presence of the Prince of Orange armed – we must surely assume that in such uncertain times, with the threat of violent attempts on William's life, openly encouraged by Philip II, hanging over him, body-searches were routine. But pistols were (as we shall see) fashion items for members of the style-conscious élite, and were worn visibly and even ostentatiously by men with military pretensions. William's closest body-guards and most trusted servants will certainly have worn them, jauntily thrust into their waistband, or hitched on to their belt (surviving pistols from this period are often provided with a belt-hook, as well as being lavishly decorated and inlaid, for orna-mental wear). Gérard's purchase of a small wheel-lock pistol within the court itself allowed him then to conceal it about his person. We may imagine the vendor will have shown him how to charge the weapon and wind the lock; all Gérard now had to do was wait for a suitable opportunity to fire it. He may have dis-charged a pistol on a previous occasion. An assassin who had never before fired a fully loaded weapon would be unlikely, even at close range, to hold steady aim under the force of the gun's unexpectedly violent recoil.

The recently-developed wheel-lock pistol was the ideal weapon to serve Gérard's purpose. It was compact and could readily be hidden in a pocket or sleeve. It was lethal at some distance from its target – like all prominent figures of the time, William will have been surrounded at all times by trusted servants who would have immediately blocked any attempt at a lunge towards him with a dagger. Above all, it could be charged with gunpowder in advance, wound up and primed, then safely carried to the scene of the crime, where it could be withdrawn and fired in a single movement. No wonder dags, in spite of their glamorous appearance and popularity as a fashion accessory among well-to-do men, rapidly acquired an association, off the battlefield, with ignominious, unheroic conduct.

Gérard was of a dour, determined temperament. He withstood torture with remarkable fortitude; nothing his interrogators tried once the deed was done could extract a confession, an admission of wrongdoing, or a plea for mercy. Unable to uncover a plot, beyond the general urgings of pamphlets and official pronouncements from the Spanish-Habsburg administration encouraging any act of violence against the Prince of Orange and promising absolution for the perpetrator, the Dutch had to make do with inflicting a carefully choreographed, appalling series of punishments on Gérard prior to execution, which was carried out in macabrely medieval fashion. The protracted physical torment of the body of the condemned man stands in stark contrast to the modernity of the way in which William had been dispatched instantaneously with the near-clinical precision of a pistol's bullet. Gérard was executed in as inhuman a manner as possible – as if his executioners were seeking some kind of comparable recompense, an equivalence of awfulness, for the unspeakable injury he had inflicted on the causes of Protestantism and nationalism in the Low Countries.

Such was the horrific cruelty of Gérard's treatment that, rather than render it yet more lurid by paraphrasing in modern English, it seems preferable to leave it to one of those in Delft at the time to provide us with an account:

> The order of the torment, and death of the murderer, was as followeth, which was four days. He had the 1st day the Strappado,* openly in the Market. The second day whipped and salted, and his right hand cut off. The third day, his breasts cut out and salt thrown in, and then his left hand cut off. The last day of his torment, which was the 10th of July, he was bound to 2 stakes, standing upright, in such order that he could not stir any way. Thus standing naked, there was a great fire placed some small distance from him, wherein was heated pincers of Iron, with which pincers, two men appointed for the same, did pinch and pull his flesh in small pieces from his bones, throughout most parts of his body. Then was he unbound from the stakes, and laid upon the earth, and again fastened to four posts, namely by his feet and arms: then they ripped up his belly at which time he had life and perfect memory, he had his bowels burned before his face, and his body cut in four several quarters. During the whole time of his execution, he remained impenitent and obstinate, rejoicing that he had slain the Prince.

According to another supposedly eyewitness account sent to the English government, Gérard conducted himself throughout his interrogation with remarkable restraint, refusing to admit any wrongdoing, 'and, what is worse, [he] desired the Prince to become a good subject to and reconcile himself to the King of Spain; and stretching out his hands to those who were watching

---

* Strappado has been described as 'the simplest form of torture'. The victim's arms are tied behind his back, and the rope securing his wrists thrown over a high beam or scaffold. He is then raised and dropped repeatedly, the rope being secured before he strikes the ground. The pain is excruciating, and eventually the victim's arms are torn from their sockets.

him and pointing at his body, exclaimed Ecce homo [Pilate's words identifying Christ before his crucifixion].' In the course of his execution itself, a minister asked him if he now repented. 'The traitor answered, "Leave me to finish my prayers", and spoke no word more, but waved his right arm and remained obstinate till death.'[28]

INDUCEMENTS FOR BOUNTY-SEEKERS

The proclamation issued by Philip II in 1580 which had incited Gérard to act, and which had explicitly urged good Catholics throughout the Habsburg Netherlands to seek every opportunity to kill the man who persisted in challenging the Habsburgs' might and right to rule, had promised:

> If there be any found, either among our own subjects, or amongst strangers, so noble of courage, and desirous of our service, and the public good, that knoweth any means how to ... set us and himself free, from [William the Silent], delivering him unto us quick or dead, or at the least taking his life from him, we will cause, to be given and provided, for him and his heirs, in good land or ready money, choose him whether, immediately after the thing shall be accomplished, the sum of 25 thousand crowns of gold.

Balthasar Gérard had evidently made his choice. Back home in Franche-Comté, his family mourned the death of their now infamous son, and like the families of suicide-bombers of today, their recompense for his 'heroism', quietly delivered some time after the event, was the massive reward in cash, lands and titles due to him under Philip II's 'Ban'.

The Ban, flagrantly placing a bounty on William's head, made the eventual assassination of William the Silent an ever-present threat and all-too-likely finale to his life. Although Gérard insisted that his motives for murdering the prince had been religious and political, and the propagandists accepted this at face value, baser motives might easily have been imputed to him.

Ever since the Ban it had been understood that there would be men committed and rash enough to take up Philip's invitation. With William's waning popularity, and a sense on all sides that he no longer had his finger on the pulse of Protestant sentiment in the Low Countries, he became more beleaguered, his entourage more fatalistic about the eventual outcome of his continuing confrontation with European Catholicism and Spanish might. In spite of all the efforts of William's followers to prevent it, it seemed to many only a matter of time before a sufficiently bold and hard-up volunteer would turn up, lured by the promise of great wealth and by the accompanying assurance of the Ban that titles and lands would, in the event of his being successful but himself dying in the attempt, be given to his immediate family.

By the time Gérard pulled out his pistol, William the Silent and his household must have been fully aware that he was likely to die a violent death in his own home. The successful assault made in July 1584 was not even the first attempt on his life by a pistol-wielding intruder. Two years earlier, William had had a remarkable – many Protestants in the Netherlands and elsewhere considered providential – escape from an uncannily similar assault, also made within the domestic space of his household and also involving a wheel-lock pistol fired at point-blank range.

3

A Miraculous Escape

Hogenburg print of Jauregay's 1582 assassination attempt on William
the Silent

IN SPRING 1582, an attempt was made on William of Orange's life at his then residence in Antwerp. Carried out by another committed adherent to the Habsburg cause, it was so nearly fatal that for weeks it was considered almost inconceivable that the prince would live. For some hours after the attack both the Duke of Anjou (who the previous year had agreed to assume the title of governor general of the United Provinces, and for William to administer the territories on his behalf) and the Spanish King Philip II (who had after all publicly offered a substantial reward to anyone who would kill the Prince of Orange) believed it had been successful. For several months afterwards the prince was confined to his palace, and in the absence of any public appearance it was widely rumoured that he was not going to survive, or was indeed already dead. The rumours and intelligence circulating across Europe threatened entirely to destabilise the region.

On Sunday, 18 March 1582, having attended morning worship in the chapel attached to his palace at Antwerp, William returned to his residence in the company of a party of noblemen and prominent figures from among the followers of the Duke of Anjou. It was Anjou's birthday, and Antwerp was in particularly festive mood. Dinner was held in public, as was customary on Sunday. The meal over, William rose from the table and walked to an alcove in the adjoining room, where he seated himself to receive a petitioner who had approached him for a favour before the meal. The man in question was an eighteen-year-old from Biscay, Jean Jauregay, a short, ill-dressed, unassuming individual with a thin black moustache, 'of face pale, drawing to a black melancholic colour'.

William believed Jauregay wished to present him with a paper; instead, he pulled out a pistol and fired it directly at the prince.

The pistol, however, had been overcharged with powder. It exploded in the assassin's hand, taking off his thumb. The force of the blast stunned the prince, seared his face, and set fire to his hair and beard. Jauregay was thrown backwards by the recoil, and the bullet veered upwards, entering the prince's neck just below the jaw, passing through his mouth, somehow without damaging either tongue or teeth, and exiting through the cheek, between jaw and ear, on the far side of his head. William later said that he was unaware of the pistol-wielding intruder, or that he had been struck by the bullet, but thought the house had collapsed on his head.

Broadsheets of the time maintained that as he fell William had cried out: 'Do not kill him! I pardon him for my death! Alas! His Highness [the Duke of Anjou] has lost a faithful servant!' It is doubtful, however, that he spoke at all – it would be some months before his doctors would allow him to communicate verbally, insisting that all his orders and instructions were issued in the form of written notes.

William's assailant stood rooted to the spot, and was cut down by multiple stab-wounds inflicted by those standing immediately around him, including William's fourteen-year-old son Maurice – a fact subsequent broadsheet (tabloid press) accounts took care to emphasise. The prince's eldest son was a prisoner of the Spanish, and did not, in any case, stand high in his father's or the Protestant cause's favour. If William died, it was generally acknowledged that Maurice would be the next in line. Although technically the stadholdership which entitled William to lead the Protestant cause in the Low Countries was an elected rather than a hereditary office, strong leadership was essential if the cause was not to collapse. Much-embellished accounts of Maurice's teenaged heroism made sure that he was the man seen as the obvious choice to succeed his father.

Word spread through Antwerp that the prince had been assassinated by French supporters of Anjou. Panic ensued, and the city teetered on the brink of lawlessness. Bands of armed Orange supporters roamed the streets looking for any Frenchmen they could find on whom to vent their fury. Anjou and his followers barricaded themselves in their lodgings. As the English agent William Herle reported to London, supporters of the Spanish cause were quick to spread the destabilising rumour that the assassination attempt had been successful, and the prince and several of his family were dead:

> The Prince of Parma hath caused Bruts [rumours] to run among his followers, that the Prince of Orange was slain outright with the Bullet, and the Princess of Pynoie to save him, was also slain, her husband hurt, and his principal Councillor run mad, both his secretaries fled to the enemy, and the rest of his people dispersed.[29]

Rumour circulated wildly. Meanwhile, across the water, English Protestants pointed the finger of blame at the Spanish for having directly encouraged the attempt on Orange's life. The Spanish ambassador in London warned Philip II:

> Your Majesty will understand by this how the venom of these people against your Majesty's interests has grown. Within a day after they learned the news about Orange they arrested

two Spanish merchants who were entering my house, on the charge that they were accomplices in the affair, which they said I had arranged . . . Leicester, whilst supping the other night with his sisters, sisters-in-law, and many kinsfolk, said openly that I had caused Orange to be shot, and that the man who shot him had been seen leaving my house a month ago . . . It is quite impossible to exaggerate the grief which the affair causes to the Queen and her ministers. They are so sad and disheartened that on the day that the news came it was the same as if she had lost the crown and they were all ruined.[30]

Within hours of the attempt it was given out that William's son Maurice had gathered up the evidence of the assailant's identity and origins. First the pistol – which had flown out of Jauregay's hand as he fired it – had been retrieved. Jauregay's body was then searched, not once, but twice. The first rummage through the dead assassin's pockets had yielded 'certain papers and booklets'. Concerned that these might be seized from them (there were those at court who believed that the assassination attempt had been made by someone close to the prince, possibly even his son), Maurice and Villiers concealed the papers and hurried with them to an upstairs room, where they opened the packet of letters and found them to be entirely in Spanish. Villiers, who now rushed to the prince's bedside, urged Maurice to look for further incriminating objects on the body. Maurice returned shortly thereafter with more papers, 'several crucifixes and Agnus Dei, a green wax candle and two bits of beaver-skin'; other reports mentioned dried toads and poison. Apparently Jauregay had been attempting to use black magic, as well as the spiritual succour of the Catholic Church, to fortify himself for his attempt on William's life.

William's senior and trusted administrator Marnix joined the group which now inspected the incriminating articles. The papers were revealed to consist of prayers and supplications. There were two bills of exchange (entirely in Spanish), one for two thousand écus, the other for 877 écus (these would, presumably, have furnished Jauregay's getaway money had he survived). The booklets were books of hours and a Jesuit catechism; there were also 'notepads covered from top to bottom in writing'.

DEAD MEN TELL NO TALES

We might reflect that Jauregay seems to have been absurdly encumbered with articles conveniently proving that the assassination attempt had been Spanish- and Catholic-backed. The hodgepodge of *objets trouvés* also apparently confirmed the fact that magic, superstition, talismans, trinkets, incantations and prayers had all played their part in the near-tragedy. Catholicism was thereby conveniently demonised as superstitious claptrap. Its adherents supposedly believed (as it was given out Jauregay did) that occult objects like those he carried would make the bearer invisible. No subsequent testimony of any of those implicated in the assassination plot ever referred to magic or witchcraft, but the litany of objects recounted in broadsheet after broadsheet and circulated around Europe took advantage of the occasion to propose a scurrilous liaison between the Catholic Church and discredited superstitious nonsense.

The bills of exchange and the bundle of letters identified Jauregay's employer as a Spanish merchant operating out of Antwerp, Gaspar de Anastro. This evidence was rushed by Marnix to Anjou, who immediately ordered that everybody at Anastro's house should be seized and questioned under threat of torture.

On their arrival the soldiers found that Anastro had left town the previous Wednesday, taking most of his possessions and sensitive business papers with him. Apparently he had had no intention of returning. Jauregay, it quickly transpired, had been Anastro's devoted servant and book-keeper. Of those still at the house, only one, twenty-year-old Antonio de Venero, like his master a native of Bilbao, turned out to have had any knowledge of the attempt Jauregay had been bent on making against the prince's life.

According to Venero's testimony – much of it extracted under torture – Anastro, formerly a wealthy and highly successful businessman, had been brought to the verge of bankruptcy by a series of losses of cargoes at sea over the preceding year. About ten months earlier, while his fortunes were still flourishing, he had been approached by Jean de Yzunça from Lisbon, who indicated that he had something of the greatest importance to communicate. After preliminary exchanges, Anastro and Yzunça began a secret correspondence – Venero was instructed not to open letters from Yzunça, and Anastro wrote the replies himself, sealing them closely. Venero had believed that the confidential matter concerned a proposed marriage arrangement between Yzunça's son and the daughter of another wealthy Spanish merchant in Antwerp, for which Anastro was being asked to help raise the dowry. In fact Yzunça had been given the mission by the King of Spain himself (or more likely the Prince of Parma) to find a well-placed Spaniard in Antwerp who would undertake to assassinate William of Orange.

Anastro's initial reaction was decisive: he turned Yzunça down flat. Shortly afterwards, however, two of Anastro's Flemish ships, laden with valuable cargo, went down on their way to Laredo, and at about the same time three ships travelling to Biscay were raided by pirates. Anastro sustained heavy losses and found himself unable to honour outstanding credit notes with Antwerp merchants as the amounts fell due. At this point Yzunça began to put pressure on Anastro to reconsider his proposal, in order to extricate himself from his acute financial embarrassment. Philip II had personally given an assurance, Yzunça wrote, that if Anastro – of whose loyalty and integrity the king had been well assured – would be given 'eighty thousand silver ducats, or property to the same value, and the Order of St. James [Jacques]'.

Unwilling to carry out the assassination himself, Anastro put the proposition first to Venero (his administrator and secretary) and then to Jean Jauregay (his junior counter-clerk), first swearing his two loyal servants to secrecy. Unfolding to them the disastrous nature of his financial predicament and the dishonour this would bring on himself and his household (weeping copiously as he did so, according to Venero's later testimony), Anastro asked whether either of them was prepared to attempt the assassination of William of Orange on his behalf. Venero declined, but Jauregay agreed, 'for the love of his master and for the honour of his name'. Anastro had treated Jauregay like one of his own family, his fortunes were entirely tied up with those of his master, and he was prepared to sacrifice himself to rescue his business and his good name. There was also a slim chance he might himself survive; although Jauregay fully expected to be seized after the attack, Anastro apparently persuaded him that the Prince of Parma would intervene directly to save his life once William was dead.

It was Anastro who had given Jauregay a pistol as the murder weapon – a handgun was too costly an item for the young book-keeper to have acquired for himself. The gun in question was one of a number of ornate, decorated dags the merchant had pur-chased to present to customers in Spain as gifts (elaborately decor-ated pistols were, as we shall see, frequently exchanged as tokens of friendship and esteem between men of means). Jauregay, however, had confided to Venero that he 'did not know how to use it'; he intended, he said, to find someone local to teach him, pretending that he himself was Flemish and thus, presumably, above suspicion.

On the Wednesday before the assassination attempt, Anastro quietly closed his Antwerp office and travelled to Bruges, en route for the safety of Catholic-controlled territory, leaving a significant number of bad debts behind him and making it clear to the remaining members of his household that he would not be returning. They expected to complete outstanding transactions, pack up their own affairs and follow. But once Anastro was safely out of Antwerp, he wrote to Jauregay instructing him to put the pre-arranged assassination plan into effect. Jauregay received the letter on the Saturday, and immediately set about finding a confessor, to gain absolution for his sins in advance of the proposed crime. He sought out a Jesuit priest who regularly held mass in Venero's house (as was permitted for foreign visitors), Antonin Temmerman, who apparently obliged.[31] The following day, Jauregay made his attempt on William's life.

The dead Jauregay could be punished no further for his misdeed. His corpse was decapitated, his body quartered and the mutilated parts prominently displayed around the Antwerp city walls. But retribution had to be exacted for so heinous a crime. Following lengthy interrogations under torture, Antonio de Venero and Antonin Temmerman were publicly executed. William intervened personally to make sure that their dispatch was swift and without undue suffering. On 28 March, therefore, they were disposed of with comparative compassion – tied to a stake on a scaffold erected in the public marketplace, their throats cut by the official executioner, their bodies quartered and displayed along with their severed heads at the gates of the city. These gruesome remains were only finally taken down when Antwerp fell to the Spanish in 1585.

MORE DEAD THAN ALIVE

Meanwhile William hovered between life and death, attended by teams of doctors and servants, and tended constantly by his devoted wife. The hole where the bullet had entered below his jaw was the size of a dollar (a large coin – something like a modern British two-pound coin). One accident of fortune was in the prince's favour: the wound had been cauterised by the explosion of the pistol, which had also set fire to William's hair and beard; this apparently prevented infection. He was also tended by two exceptionally able physicians: an Antwerp surgeon named Gaspar, and the Duke of Anjou's doctor, Votallys, who specialised in bullet wounds, 'whereof he has written a treatise'.

Three days after the event it seemed unlikely the prince could survive. William Herle reported to London:

> It is thought by Gasper the surgeon, who has charge (among others) of the Prince's wound, that he cannot escape, for that the artery is touched, and accidents do increase that make the cure out of hope, though better speech [more positive accounts] be blown abroad.[32]

The inside of William's mouth had swollen badly, making it difficult for the doctors to assess the internal damage. He was being given as little nourishment as possible, in case this might cause a 'canker' or gangrene to develop. William continued to bleed copiously, and the doctors staunched the flow with pads of lint cloth.

The prince was apparently a man of remarkably strong constitution. By 28 April Herle was able to report that William had regained his power of speech:

> The Prince of Orange (thanks be to almighty God, by whose miracle he is preserved) is able to walk in his chamber, with whom I was this afternoon & Colonel Morgan with me, being heartily demanded by the said Prince how your honor, the Lord Treasurer & the Earl of Leicester did, speaking unto me without impediment of tongue: some little contusion, yet remains, which is hoped to become better shortly.[33]

By 25 May those close to the Orange circle like Herle could report that there was a significant further improvement in the prince's condition:

> The Prince's wound shows good appearance of amendment, but till the seventh day be past (which determines about one of the clock this Sunday) and the ninth day also, no full assurance can be made, though his friends be of the opinion that the danger is past. The Prince is of such courage that it makes the care easier in him, that would be impossible in a weaker person.

Further from the court, however, the continued sequestration of the convalescent prince fuelled persistent rumours that he had succumbed to his wound. A week before Herle's optimistic report another Continental spy informed Walsingham that it was being reported that William had finally died of his injuries.[34]

There were indeed some dramatic setbacks. On several occasions bleeding recommenced, in spite of the fact that William's servants took it in turns to apply pressure to the vulnerable spot with a 'tent' or lint swab, held in place by one finger, night and day. One of these lint swabs was mislaid inside the wound and could not be found for twelve days. William's surgeons were reluctant to allow the wound to heal over in the meantime, anticipating that it would eventually break open again to expel the extraneous matter, or that surgical intervention might be required once it was located. The swab eventually turned up, and healing was allowed to continue.

Against all the odds, William made a complete recovery. It was his wife now, weakened by weeks of tending to him, who succumbed to a sickness of her own. On 4 May 1582 the Prince of Orange was at last well enough to appear in public, at a service of thanksgiving held for his recovery in the church attached to his residence. The very next day, however, it was announced that his wife, the Princess of Orange, had died. The court was plunged into official mourning, passing seamlessly from the state of inaction occasioned by the prince's drawn-out illness, to that required following the death of a member of the prince's close family.

DAMAGING UNCERTAINTY

By 1580 William of Orange's reputation for hedging his bets was proving increasingly unhelpful in the international arena. The political power struggle between Europe's Protestant and Catholic powers was being fought out on Low Countries soil, but William's vacillation over which power to enlist on Holland's side against the Spanish had led to a virtual stalemate in which Spanish forces were reduced to fighting a defensive war against troops surreptitiously funded and reinforced by England, Germany and Protestant France. This support ebbed and flowed with the exigencies of internal politics in these European countries, without there being any consistent strategy or policy to guide them on the ground.

William's campaign planning was hampered by the uncertainties of supply and finance, and no clear way forward appears to have emerged. Even William's remarkable ability to survive a pistol fired in his face at point-blank range only added to the political uncertainty. In spite of his extraordinary physical resilience and his doctors' exceptionally competent treatment, it was still not clear that William would not succumb to a complication or infection, nor was it certain that if he did survive, his health would permit him to continue to act as the Protestant cause's military commander and political figurehead in the northern Netherlands.

In the face of deepening scepticism over the Prince of Orange's ability to lead the Protestant states effectively, the prolonged period of recuperation necessitated by his terrible wound, followed by the further period of retreat from public life required by decorum after the death of the princess, further aggravated political uncertainty. William's enforced absence from the public scene threatened the carefully-constructed alliance of interests against the occupying forces of the Habsburg Emperor Philip II in the Netherlands with collapse. The flimsy accord between the Orangists, the English and the French relied upon William's personality, the confidence he inspired, and his proven track record in standing firm against the might of the Habsburgs.

In the days following the assassination attempt, the States General went into suspended animation and would enact no new legislation while it was unclear whether William would survive. Government in the United Provinces ground to a halt. The attack also came at a critical moment in negotiations between the Prince of Orange (on behalf of the States General) and the French Duke of Anjou, over the latter's assumption of the title and office of governor general of the United Provinces. With the prince out of action and apparently on his deathbed, the already lukewarm support for the Duke of Anjou – French, and a Catholic – virtually evaporated. Herle reported:

> Touching Monsieur [Anjou], he applies his business here with marvellous care and travail, and yet can bring them to no resolution or certainty for their finances (which are the ground of all) before they do see that the Prince of Orange will live or die.

Even once William was out of immediate danger, it proved difficult to rebuild confidence in his carefully-brokered plan to install Anjou as the figurehead to stand up against Philip II's claims to sovereignty over the Low Countries. The alliance with the French had required strong Dutch leadership to see it through. Now that that was no longer available, Anjou's unreliability, and Dutch distaste for any kind of agreement with the French (particularly a Catholic Frenchman), once again became topics for debate. Writing to Walsingham in late April, Herle expressed the view that the prince was unlikely ever to regain his former strength, and that even if he made a full recovery, 'he shall yet hardly have the vigour of mind and senses that he had before'. The English government must therefore remain vigilant, he counselled, in case others began to interfere in affairs of state in William's name.

4

The Wheel-Lock Pistol –
Killing Conveniently

PISTOL POWER ON THE BATTLEFIELD

THE WHEEL-LOCK MECHANISM for firing a portable firearm efficiently was one of the landmark technological innovations of the early sixteenth century. In terms of its transformative impact on developments reaching far beyond its immediate military context, it matches the pocket watch, which uses a closely similar mechanism.

The handgun's wheel-lock mechanism consists of a hard, steeled disk of 25–40 millimetres in diameter, which is made to rotate by means of a coiled spring. The spring drives the 'wheel' mechanism. The spring is wound up by hand in advance and held in readiness until released by a trigger. Alongside the spring-loaded wheel, the other crucial part of the mechanism is a miniature clamp at the end of a movable arm holding a piece of hard stone, usually iron pyrites. When the spring is released, a series of gears sets the wheel turning, and sparks are struck at the point of contact between the spinning wheel and the pyrites, as in a traditional cigarette lighter. The wheel is mounted inside a powder pan, usually a block of metal with an enclosed cavity containing fine-grained priming gunpowder, and this communicates with the main powder charge through a touchhole in the gun barrel.

The wheel-lock pistol is a labour- and technology-intensive instrument of warfare. Both Italians and Germans claimed it as their invention, but once its design was perfected it caught on so quickly that it is hard to judge whether it was a Nuremberger or

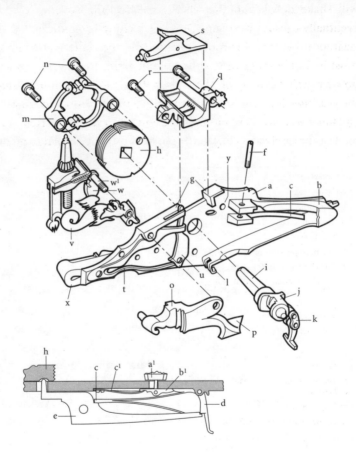

The wheel-lock mechanism of a sixteenth-century pistol

perhaps even that greatest of all artist-designers Leonardo da Vinci (as some gun experts claim) who first thought of it.

A working wheel-lock requires great precision during the manufacturing process. Because the wheel intrudes into the powder pan, clearances between the wheel and the slot within which it spins must be small, otherwise the fine-grained priming powder will shake down into the wheel's mechanism, slowing it and eventually causing it to jam. One recent study has indicated that clearances between the moving wheel and the static metal block must be in the range of 0.04–0.08 millimetres to prevent primer powder grains (averaging about 0.1 millimetres) from infiltrating the gear housing. The spring, its winding mechanism and trigger, and any covers to keep out moisture and dust therefore have to be made as precisely as a clock or fine lock, yet still be rugged enough

a Lockplate	p Mainspring stop on o
b Mainspring	q Pan, slotted for the wheel and the edge of the lockplate to which it is attached at g
c Sear-spring	
d Trigger-lever	r Retaining screws for q
e Sear-lever	s Sliding pan-cover pivoted to the top of u
f Sear pivot-pin securing sear-lever to y	t Pan-cover spring
g Shoulders on which the pan q is supported	u Pan-cover arm, pivoted at the bottom
h Wheel with square hole for the spindle i and circular recess in which the nose of the sear e engages	v Cock, the neck chiselled in the form of a wyvern. The lower jaw of the dog-head is movable
i Wheel-spindle	w Cock bridle
j Portion of i round which the transmission-chain k winds	w¹ Cock-spring
k Transmission-chain terminating in a toggle that engages with the mainspring at l	y Lugs between which the sear-lever e is pivoted. The upper one also serves to secure the end of the mainspring
l End of mainspring shaped to receive the toggle on k	a¹ External knob of sliding safety-catch
m Ring-shaped wheel-cover	b¹ Safety-catch lever which engages over the toe of the trigger-lever d
n Screws for attaching m to the lockplate	c¹ Safety-catch spring
o Bridle supporting the inner end of the wheel-spindle i with mainspring stop at p	

for field service. The trick to fabricating the mechanism was discovered early in the sixteenth century: to use the wheel as a cutter to mill its own slot in the powder pan.[35] As with a clock, too, the wheel-lock gun had to be maintained by a skilled craftsman to keep it in good working order. Once in use, the mechanism had to be kept scrupulously clean to avoid its seizing up.

Nevertheless, use of the wheel-lock pistol spread across Europe with remarkable rapidity during the second half of the sixteenth century. The obvious attraction of the wheel-lock mechanism was that it removed the need to stop and prepare the weapon for firing within sight of the enemy. It could be loaded and primed ahead of use, then discharged when needed using only one hand. Unlike the arquebus – which had to be fired with a smouldering taper – the wheel-lock gun could be conveniently used from horseback. Pistols rapidly became the firearm used in battle by light horse infantrymen. The horseman might carry three or more primed pistols into action – one in his hand and two attached to his belt or in saddle-holsters. Some accounts set the number at six, with an additional two pistols stuffed into the rider's boots, and one more behind him in the saddle. According to one leading expert in military history, light horsemen replaced heavy cavalry in western Europe in the second half of the sixteenth century as a direct result of the invention of the wheel-lock pistol.[36]

'The horse-mounted pistoleer was able to match the traditional man-at-arms in terms of mobility while outranging him in striking power. Against infantrymen, traditional heavy cavalry could adopt a number of tactical stances that served to maintain some aspects of cavalry's former pre-eminence on the field of battle. Faced with mounted pistoleers, the heavy cavalryman was confronted with a pressing and often lethal threat; the only choice was to adapt by imitation.'[37] The era of the mounted knight in battle in full armour was brought to a close by the handgun.

Wheel-lock handguns began to appear on the battlefield in substantial numbers in the 1540s. Horsemen whose main weapon was the pistol were known as *Reiters* – that is, 'riders'; in French, *reîtres*; in Italian, *raitri*. These riders were members of light cavalry units. Their mounts had to be quick to manage and turn, unlike the usual thundering, carthorse-like heavy cavalry. Soldiers had to be considerable horsemen to act as *reiters* or pistoleers: the manoeuvres required for effective use of pistols in battle involved a close formation of rows of horsemen who rode fast, directly at the enemy, fired at close range and then wheeled away so that the row of men behind could do the same. Pistoleers' attempts to use their weapons against infantry formations involved a form of manoeuvre known as the *caracole* or *limaçon*, in which successive ranks of horsemen moved forward to within striking distance, wheeled their horses right or left as circumstances dictated, fired pistol shots into the formed infantry ranks, and then retired to reload.[38]

In English these engagements were referred to as 'skirmishes'. When a contemporary account of a battle describes infantrymen or heavy cavalry being involved in a skirmish it refers to the fact that a reasonably static body of men armed with pikes and slow-to-fire arquebuses joins battle with a much more manoeuvrable group of fast-moving cavalry, whose pistol-fire inflicts its damage from just outside the range of pikes and lances. Sir Philip Sidney, darling of the English Protestant cause and a favourite of Queen Elizabeth's, was fighting as a *reiter* in a skirmish with Spanish troops when he received his fatal wound at the Battle of Zutphen.[39] We may take him as a typical wheel-lock-pistol-wielding adversary in battle. High-born and a consummate horseman, the role of *reiter* perfectly suited his modern techno-logically-savvy sensibility, combined with an old-style chivalric ethic of warfare.

Describing the novelty of *reiter* tactics in the 1580s, the distinguished military strategist François de la Noue devoted an entire chapter of his treatise on warfare to the 'paradox' that a squadron of *reiters* could outmanoeuvre a comparable squadron of infantry-men equipped with lances:

> Although the squadrons of the lances do give a gallant charge, yet it can work no great effect, for at the outset it killeth none, yea it is a miracle if any be slain with the spear. Only it may wound some horse, and as for the shock, it is many times of small force, whereas the perfect Reiter do never discharge their pistols but in joining, and striking close at hand, they wound, aiming always either at the face or the thigh. The second rank also shooteth off so that the forefront of the men-of-arms squadron is at the first meeting half overthrown and maimed. Although the first rank may with their lances do some hurt, especially to the horses, yet the other ranks following cannot do so, or at the least only the second and third, but are driven to cast away their spears and to help themselves with their swords . . . I am driven to avow that a squadron of pistols, doing their duties, shall break a squadron of lances.[40]

What de la Noue was responding to here was the impact of the wheel-lock handgun on the whole way warfare was then conducted. The views he expresses in his treatise were of particular interest to the English in the period, because de la Noue was something of a celebrity there for his services to the Protestant cause. In 1577 this French Huguenot tactician intercepted letters from the Habsburg regent in the Low Countries to the Spanish king containing a plot to poison Elizabeth and marry Mary Stuart to Philip of Spain's half-brother. De la Noue sent the letters to William of Orange, who passed them to one of Walsingham's Low Countries agents.[41] Between 1578 and 1580 (when he was captured in battle, not being released until after William's death, in 1585) de la Noue was a senior member of William of Orange's administration, and a key figure in his military campaign. England's leading military commander, Sir John Norris, co-commanded William of Orange's forces with de la Noue in the Low Countries campaigns in 1579.[42]

Prominent military men of the second half of the sixteenth century, like de la Noue, Sir John Norris and Norris's colleague and sometime competitor for control of English forces Sir Roger Williams – all of whom fought for the Protestant cause against the Spanish in the Low Countries – express enthusiasm for the strategic advantage of pistols on the battlefield. 'Without a doubt, the Pistoll discharged hard by, well charged and with judgement, murthers more than the Launce,' wrote Williams in his *Briefe Discourse of War* (1590). Williams knew about pistol skirmishes – he had been knighted alongside the Earl of Essex after the Battle of Zutphen in 1586, for courageous conduct in the very skirmish in which that other pistol-bearing soldier, Sir Philip Sidney, was fatally wounded.

This enthusiasm for pistol warfare had a good deal to do with the kind of European campaigns in which these men saw active service. Required to harry and harass the Spanish troops both while they were on the move and during one of their many sieges of fortified Dutch towns, the light horse *reiters* had clear advantages. In this context, *reiters* with their pistols figure much like the seaborne privateers who during the same campaigns harried Spanish ships along the northern coast of the Netherlands, using similar tactics of speed and surprise. Both Norris's and Williams's colourful contemporary printed accounts of their military careers include descriptions of skirmish engagements, in the course of which both received pistol-shot wounds (on one occasion Norris received a painful gunshot wound in the buttocks).[43]

De la Noue's acknowledgement of the swift impact of wheel-lock weaponry on military tactics is particularly telling in view of the fact that patterns of warfare otherwise evolved extremely slowly over the fifteenth and sixteenth centuries. The introduction of guns and gunpowder apparently altered traditional patterns of engagement rather little. As one of the foremost modern authorities on warfare in the period observes: 'Artillery in the fifteenth century and the wheel-lock pistol in the sixteenth are model cases of how technology can alter longstanding habits in fairly short order. But if one looks at the larger patterns of technological change over a longer time span, an ironic twist emerges. Although the transformation of military operations in the sixteenth century is usually attributed to technological and tactical innovations, what actually happened was a form of tactical stasis rooted in a lack of further technological change.'[44] The arrival of the handgun dramatically altered the deployment of troops in battle, and this was clearly understood by tacticians with experience in the military arena in the Low Countries in the late 1570s and 1580s.[45] Thereafter, tactics remained relatively unchanged for another century.

Finally, there was a connection between the spread of manufacture of wheel-lock pistols and the unstable political situation throughout Europe. In the second half of the sixteenth century England offered sanctuary for a steady stream of refugees from the religious wars in mainland Europe, many of whom were skilled craftsmen. In the inventory of gunsmiths working in London in the period, most come originally from the Netherlands, or more rarely from France and Germany.[46] Having been developed in the context of actual warfare on the European mainland, wheel-lock pistols were soon being produced for the home market in England, where they became equally popular among military men and those wishing to provide themselves with personal protection.

GUN CULTURE

A handgun features as a status accessory in a significant number of portraits from the last quarter of the sixteenth century. Because of its clearly portable nature as a fire-arm, the pistol figures in English Elizabethan portraiture as one of the emblematic attributes of the military man on the move. Thomas Cockson's 1599 engraving of Robert Devereux, 2nd Earl of Essex, as 'God's elected' (see next page), against a background representing various arenas of war in which he led troops sponsored by Elizabeth I on behalf of the Protestant cause, shows him seated on a small, fast horse, with his baton of command in his right hand, while his left holds the butt of a pistol in an elaborate holster attached to his saddle. Behind him, troops exchange gunfire.[47]

Soldiers closely associated with Elizabethan campaigns in Ireland similarly affect a pistol as part of the insignia representing their military role there. Once again, the terrain and the nature of the conflict favoured small contingents of mobile troops over the set-piece formations backed up by heavy guns of traditional campaigns.

In the well-known portrait by Marcus Gheeraerts the younger of Captain Thomas Lee (1594, see p. 87), now in the Tate Britain Gallery in London, the combination of indigenous costume and

The Earl of Essex equipped for a skirmish

technically sophisticated portable weaponry announces Lee's position as belonging to the kind of mobile forces on whom English limited success against the guerrilla tactics of the native Irish forces depended. Lee is dressed in 'native' fashion as an indigenous

Captain Thomas Lee with his pistol prominently displayed

Irish fighter, but he wears a lavishly decorated state-of-the-art wheel-lock pistol at his waist, attached to his belt with a belt-hook. A Latin inscription on the tree behind him compares him to the loyal Roman, Mucius Scaevola, who infiltrated the ranks of the enemy in disguise, implying that Lee too will serve Queen Elizabeth faithfully. In this highly contrived and self-conscious composition, Lee's 'disguise' as an Irishman is deliberately contrasted with the highly visible, centrally placed modern weapon of war.[48]

Elizabeth I's great favourite (and one-time suitor) Robert Dudley, Earl of Leicester, chose to have his portrait painted with a gun as a prominent accessory in place of a baton of command at least twice. Both portraits followed his appointment by the queen in 1585 to lead the disastrous campaign to assist the Dutch Protestant cause in the Low Countries. This was a campaign which came about as a direct result of William the Silent's assassination, and to which we will return. During it, Leicester (on the advice of his general, Sir John Norris) adopted *reiters* and skirmishing as a strategic part of his battlefield tactics in engagements on difficult terrain, where surprise was of the essence, and where he knew from the outset that his forces were bound to be significantly outnumbered by their Spanish opponents.

Leicester's accounts for 1584–86 (the period prior to and during his Low Countries campaign) record him purchasing a number of pistols. For example, in June 1585, while he awaited his Low Countries command from the queen and was making ready troops and equipment in order to be able to leave at a moment's notice, Leicester paid Robert Gwin three pounds for '2 cases of pistols and their furniture', and a further sum of six shillings for 'mending of the damask case of pistols'.[49] Another case of pistols with a spanner, horn and other accessories cost him one pound ten shillings.

Robert Dudley, Earl of Leicester,
leaning on a wheel-lock gun

These are relatively expensive items. There are also payments for the essential upkeep required to keep pistols in full working order – a payment of twenty shillings, for instance, 'unto Lewes for mending your lordship's dagg'.[50]

While Leicester lingered in England, waiting for Elizabeth to make up her mind to send him to command her forces in the Low Countries, Sir John Norris had already embarked in September, in anticipation of a decision which had been virtually inevitable since the key port of Antwerp fell to the Spanish in August, and was doing a brisk business in fire-arms as part of the equipping of the seven thousand men he had brought with him. In fact, Norris was making a handsome profit, by deducting a sum from each soldier's pay for his equipment, estimating the cost at English prices, then purchasing locally in the Netherlands where weapons were significantly cheaper, and pocketing the difference.[51]

Leicester's command in the Low Countries ended ignominiously in 1587. The so-called Parham portrait (now at Parham House), painted after his return, and after he had relinquished the title of governor general, bestowed on him by the States of Holland in 1586, shows him with his hand covering the muzzle of his up-ended wheel-lock gun. Faced with loss of face and the queen's displeasure, there is no mistaking the symbolic acknowledgement of lost virility and manhood brought low.

The obvious lewd possibilities where pistols were depicted in paintings require that the pistol rests jauntily in the sitter's lap, or is held cocked upwards in his hand (as the baton of command is similarly angled in pictures representing leadership). Semantics supported such visual innuendo. The words 'pistol' and 'pizzle' (penis) invited puns, even without the visual similarities between gun and male organ. This raises the serious possibility that in late-Elizabethan England, pistols might have been understood as symbols of a potency, valour and martial prowess which the female monarch was all too clearly lacking. If so, there may be a correlation between portraits in which pistols appear prominently, and their sitters' association with the circle at the English court which was discontented with the queen's policy of avoiding military confrontation in Europe.

Whether or not they were conscious of the symbolism of the weapons they clutched, jauntily erect, men who chose to portray themselves holding a pistol do appear to want to convey their link to the military, and the so-called 'war party' led by Burghley, Leicester and Walsingham. The case of Sir William Stanley will stand here for all the gentleman soldiers who participated in the Irish and Low Countries campaigns, and who also chose to portray themselves as above all pistol-bearing men.

Sir William Stanley was kinsman to Edward Stanley, Earl of Derby, whose service he entered in the 1560s. Soon afterwards, he crossed to the Spanish Netherlands and began his illustrious military career. He had been raised as a Catholic, and to begin with was a volunteer under Alva fighting for the Spanish, but in 1570 he left the Low Countries and joined Elizabeth's forces in Ireland. Although he kept his Catholic conviction he served as a soldier in Ireland for fifteen years, distinguishing himself in the campaign and gaining a knighthood for his bravery. In 1584 he was badly wounded and returned to England.

In early 1586 the Earl of Leicester, from the Netherlands, petitioned to be allowed to order Stanley to join him, bringing with him a thousand men recruited by Stanley from the Irish forces of his previous command. Stanley eventually joined Leicester in August. He and his troops fought at the Battle of Zutphen, where Sir Philip Sidney received his fatal wounds. In an engagement in which Leicester's forces turned out to be badly outnumbered, it was Stanley and his Irish soldiers who seized some of the Spanish wagons, while Norris tried to obtain reinforcements. When these were not forthcoming, Norris and Stanley organised a tactical withdrawal, thereby saving most of the light horse troop which had made the first assault, and which included a number of prominent young English nobles, including the Earl of Essex and Sir Philip Sidney.

Thereafter Stanley's career was somewhat less glorious. Having failed to relieve Zutphen, Leicester decided to blockade the city, and gave Stanley the command of the strategically important town of Deventer close by. Leicester meanwhile returned to England for the winter. On 21 January Norris wrote to the Privy Council informing them that Stanley had surrendered Deventer to the Spanish and gone over to the Spanish side himself, and that the outer works blockading Zutphen had also been yielded without a struggle. On top of its devastating consequences for the English campaign at Zutphen, Stanley's defection badly damaged Leicester's command in the eyes of the Dutch.[52]

Sir William Stanley was by no means the only soldier to fight on both sides during the Dutch Revolt. Professional soldiers might go into battle for whoever was prepared to pay them. It is as a professional soldier in the Irish and Low Countries wars that Stanley has himself represented in two surviving portraits, in elaborate, customised armour, proudly holding his pistol erect and cocked across his lap.

USED IN SELF-DEFENCE

In the Low Countries in particular an association with pistols underscores the hands-on nature of the conflict, even for the commander, and the personal heroism of the individual soldier. It is also the weapon of both attack and self-defence in what were effectively the civil-war circumstances which prevailed in Ireland, France and the Low Countries throughout the 1570s and '80s. Graphic contemporary news-style engravings of both the St Bartholomew's Day massacre in Paris (1572) and the so-called 'French Fury' unleashed by the Duke of Anjou in Antwerp in January 1583 show hand-to-hand fighting in which handguns figure prominently.[53]

In spite of its impact on the battlefield, there was from the start a certain ambiguity as to whether the wheel-lock pistol was an élite weapon or a 'low' underhand one. Unlike any other fire-arm, the pistol could be kept concealed, then produced and fired without warning. It was rapidly adopted by those conducting robbery with threats – armed robbers, highwaymen or assassins. As early as 1518 the Emperor Maximilian banned the manufacture and possession of 'self-igniting handguns that set themselves to firing' anywhere within the Habsburg empire. In 1542 Venice banned all guns small enough to be concealed in a sleeve. In 1532 the Nuremberg city council complained that although law-abiding citizens were not allowed to own wheel-lock handguns, highwaymen and robbers all carried them, so that the law was unenforceable.

When the French essayist Michel de Montaigne was thrown from his horse in a freak accident during the French civil wars, he naturally assumed, when he regained consciousness, that he had been the victim of an attack by a gunman, appearing out of the blue on horseback.[54]

In English stage drama of the period, pistols are the weapons of surprise favoured by conspirators and murderers. Above all, they are regarded as instruments of treachery and deception. In John Webster's *The White Devil* (1609–12), Flamineo hands his sister Vittoria – the unscrupulous woman of the play's title – two boxed pairs of pistols and suggests that they commit double suicide:

> . . . *take these pistols,*
> *Because my hand is stained with blood already:*
> *Two of these you shall level at my breast,*
> *The other 'gainst your own, and so we'll die*
> *Most equally contented.*

Vittoria and her maid each discharge a pistol at Flamineo, who falls to the ground. While they, however, rejoice at outwitting him, he leaps to his feet and denounces them, declaring that 'The pistols held no bullets: 'twas a plot/To prove your kindness to me; and I live/To punish your ingratitude . . . How cunning you were to discharge!'[55] Cunning, dissimulation, ignoble conduct – all these are associated with the person who carries a handgun into a private house with the intention of causing harm to one of its inmates.

Use of pistols thematically to underscore roguery and deception is not confined to the stage, but occurs also in popular prose. In Thomas Nashe's picaresque tale of deception and betrayal, *The Unfortunate Traveller* (1593), pistols crop up as a sort of running refrain on the hidden dangers that lie in wait for the incautious traveller – each pistol surfacing as evidence of betrayal and skulduggery. As the climax of these encounters, the tale's hero,

Jack Wilton, himself almost succumbs to a plot hatched by a Venetian courtesan named Tabitha, who together with her pimp tries to tempt Jack's servant Brunquel into murdering his master in exchange for her favours and a supposed fortune in gold:

> Now (quoth she), if you be disposed to make him away in their absence, you shall have my house at command. Stab, poison, or shoot him through with a pistol, all is one; into the vault he shall be thrown when the deed is done. On my bare honesty, it was a crafty quean [whore], for she had enacted with herself, if he had been my legitimate servant, as he was one that served and supplied my necessities, when he had murdered me, to have accused him of the murder, and made all that I had hers (as I carried all my master's wealth, money, jewels, rings, or bills of exchange, continually about me).
>
> He very subtly consented to her stratagem at the first motion; kill me he would, that heavens could not withstand, and a pistol was the predestinate engine which must deliver the parting blow.

The trusty Brunquel, however, reveals the plot to his master, and they devise a plan to unmask the villainous pair. On the day chosen to carry out the murder, as Brunquel enters Jack's bedroom (carrying his pre-charged pistol) with the conspirators hard on his heels, Jack starts up in bed, announcing that he has just had an extraordinary dream:

> I dreamt, quoth I, that my man Brunquel here (for no better name got he of me) came into my chamber with a pistol charged under his arm to kill me, and that he was suborned by you, Mistress Tabitha, and my very good friend, Petro de Campo Frego [her pimp]; God send it turn to good, for it hath affrighted me above measure.

Tabitha and Petro are all ready to bluster their way out of the situation, but by a prearranged ruse Brunquel 'as it was before compacted between us, let his pistol drop from him on the sudden, wherewith I started out of my bed, and drew my rapier, and cried, Murder, murder, which made goodwife Tabitha ready to bepiss her'.

> My servant, or my master, which you will, I took roughly by the collar, and threatened to run him through incontinent if he confessed not the truth. He, as it were, stricken with remorse of conscience (God be with him, for he could counterfeit most daintily), down on his knees, asked me forgiveness, and impeached Tabitha and Petro de Campo Frego as guilty of subornation.

Wilton agrees not to turn his would-be assailants in to the authorities on a charge of conspiracy to murder, in exchange for a large amount of gold coin (which naturally turns out subsequently to be counterfeit). In the world of tabloid-style rogues, pistols and bedrooms are the stuff sensational stories are made of.

ÉLITE TOYS AND FASHIONABLE ACCESSORIES

The pistol was a lethal weapon, but it quickly proved to be a highly coveted and collectible object. The intrinsic beauty of handguns, their technical sophistication and the lavishness with which individual guns were ornamented in the course of manufacture (using all the skills of the clock- and lock-maker's art) lent themselves to display in a rich man's armoury. The Habsburg Emperor Charles V boasted a large personal collection of handguns, including many ornate and complex wheel-lock examples.

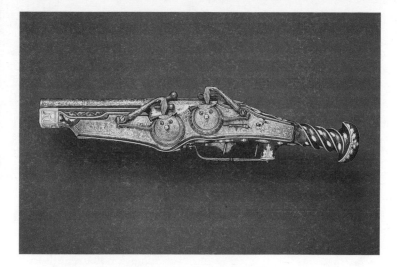

Double-barrelled wheel-lock pistol of Emperor Charles V, *ca.* 1540–45.
Made by Peter Peck (1500/10–1596). German (Munich).
Steel, etched and gilded; wood inlaid with engraved staghorn;
length 19⅜ in. (49.2 cm)

The expense involved in the wheel-lock pistol's production meant that it invited further skilled attention in the form of fine decoration. Accordingly, the barrel and lock-plate, as well as the lock itself, the belt-hook (if the weapon had one) and the trigger guard were all frequently lavishly ornamented, with damascening in gold and silver applied to the steel of the weapon.

In the example illustrated above (one of Charles V's wheel-lock pistols, with two separate mechanisms for firing the two barrels), the pistol is decorated with Charles's dynastic and personal emblems: the double-headed imperial eagle and the pillars of Hercules with the Latin motto '*Plus ultra*'. A surviving example from the 1590s, now in the Victoria and Albert Museum in London (shown on the cover of this volume), is decorated with a seated, helmeted female figure with trophies on the lock-plate, classical figures on the barrel, together with trophies, helmets and fruit, and scrolling foliage, acanthus, snails, dragonflies, birds, butterflies and fruit on remaining areas.[56]

In the sixteenth century as now, handguns held a special place in popular affection – 'boys' toys' to be coveted, admired and, on both appropriate and inappropriate occasions, fired, in anger or in self-defence. At a glance the pistol-carrier could convey machismo, masculinity, bravura and fear. A heady and volatile mix of beauty and danger, violence and reassurance, then as now, gave the pistol its peculiar fascination.

5

English Aftermath 1 –
'She is a Chief Mark they Shoot at'

COPYCAT CONSPIRACIES AND
HIDDEN HANDGUNS

This Pope doth send Magicians to her land
To seek her death, by that their devilish art:
Yea which is more, he'd cause a devilish dolt
Of France, a Doctor (Parry I do mean)
With smiling face for to discharge a Dag [pistol]
At her kind heart, who saved had his life.[57]

BETWEEN THE TWO ATTEMPTS on the life of William of
Orange in 1582 and 1584 – the providential escape and the fatal
wounding – there was growing concern amongst Elizabeth I's
ministers and advisers that a similar Spanish-backed assassination
attempt would be made against the queen.

England's intelligence agents abroad emphasised in their dispatches that the daring of the attempts against William were likely
to encourage Elizabeth's enemies to try to eliminate her next, by
similar means. Three days after Jauregay's attempt on William's life,
William Herle wrote to the Earl of Leicester from Antwerp insisting
that the English queen was now in mortal danger. At this stage it
was widely believed that Prince William was unlikely to survive.

Queen Elizabeth herself would be the next victim of an assassination, warned Herle from the Low Countries, and he pointed an accusing finger directly at the Spanish ambassador in London:

> There is an advertisement given by a counsellor of importance here, that there is somewhat practised against her Majesty's person in England by Bernardine de Mendoza [the Spanish ambassador], whereof if there be particularities, I shall with the care and duty that becomes me, advertise by special messenger what is certain on that behalf.

English agents in the Low Countries were particularly concerned to make it clear at home that the Spanish threat was no less grave in London than in Antwerp, even though the Dutch were in active rebellion against Spain, whereas England had for years been carefully withholding its official support from either side in the conflict. According to the agents, it was widely believed in mainland Europe that England might slide into civil war at any moment. In May 1582, Herle – affecting grave concern – reported to Walsingham that it was being put about in Antwerp that Catholic factions in England were massing against the queen, and that England would soon be at war with France:

> Here is a great brut [noise], which is grounded upon advertisements come to Monsieur [Anjou], that England is in arms against the Queen. The papists grown strong. The Queen perplexed with force and difficulty. The Earls of Leicester and Sussex banded in great troops one against another, both of them commanded to their houses. Mr Hatton and the Earl of Sussex become Spanish, yourself [Walsingham] in fear to fall with the Earl of Leicester, great leagues made among the nobility and those particularly named.

'The time is come that the Queen must know her self to be but a woman, and to have need of a head to govern things,' writes

Herle. He insists that surveillance measures are needed to stop conspirators and assassins entering England too (his alarmism is uncannily reminiscent of twenty-first-century responses to the threat of international terrorism):

> Finally that the passages and ports of England be shut up, guarded with officers who search every man to the soles of the shoes for letters and papers of conspiracy and rebellion. Of all which the States General have been informed particularly by the French, they even sitting in Council, which as I guess is to alienate their minds and good opinions from England, and to turn their course by sinister degrees another way.

In dispatches like these Herle singled out for particularly vigilant scrutiny individuals travelling to London from the European mainland on diplomatic business, in case they should turn out to be would-be assassins. It was, of course, part of Herle's job as an intelligencer to contribute to a heightened sense of anxiety about what might happen should intelligence-gatherers like himself fail to anticipate even the most far-fetched of potential dangers. Thus in November 1583 he warned Lord Burghley:

> Don Gaston that is come from the Prince of Parma, to go into Spain to the King from hence is a man reputed of action, of the age of 33 years, and hath but one eye, and very resolute. His Father was a Genoese, his mother a Spaniard and by his country a Sicilian which is the worst commixture that ever was, and therefore for God's sake, let him be well observed. For tomorrow is a solemn day, which ought not to be without care of her Majesty's security, her person being the highest Jewel that Christendom now hath. Those solemn days have bred danger many times beside that the coming of this man at this instant hither, his conditions also weighed, hath made me never cease till I had uttered in

humble zeal this my conceit to your good Lord, and so most
humbly I take my leave.[58]

When William eventually fell to an assassin's bullet in 1584, the
English response was once again to imagine that an attempt would
most likely follow against the life of Queen Elizabeth. A week
after the assassination, Sir Edward Stafford wrote to Walsingham
from Paris urgently informing him that 'the same practice that
hath been executed on the Prince of Orange' was likely to be used
against the queen:

> Don Antonio sent that last day in haste for me, and, with
> his affection to the Queen, declared to me a very certain
> advertisement he had out of a very good place, and out of
> the Spanish Agent's house besides, that the same practice
> that hath been executed on the Prince of Orange, there are
> practices more than two or three about to execute it upon
> her Majesty and some others within these two months. I
> have had like advertisements by other means.
>
> There is no doubt that she is a chief mark they shoot at,
> and seeing there were men cunning enough to enchant a
> man, and to encourage one to kill the Prince of Orange in
> the midst of Holland, and a knave found desperate enough
> to do it, we must think that hereafter anything may be done.
> God preserve her Majesty.[59]

Two or three attempts are in train against the life of the most
powerful remaining figurehead of the Protestant cause in Europe
– the Queen of England. 'She is a chief mark they shoot at' carries
the clear assumption that what is expected is another audacious
assassination attempt with a pistol.

There were political motives behind these claimed conspiracies
and death threats. After William's assassination the Leicester faction at the English court believed that the queen would now
have to intervene to support William and his Protestant United

Elizabeth I, reluctant champion of
the Dutch Protestant cause

Provinces against imperial Catholic Habsburg aggression. Elizabeth herself was still equally determined to avoid direct military confrontation with Philip II, which would incur huge expenditure and long-running warfare whose outcome was unpredictable. Both in 1582 and 1584 the assaults on the Prince of Orange triggered Elizabeth's chief war-party ministers to bring pressure to bear on her to intervene in the conflict between the States General and the Spanish crown. In March 1582, when Herle believed that William was unlikely to survive the first assassination attempt, he took the opportunity to make an urgent request that English troops be sent to help restore order. On that occasion his alarmed appeal for English intervention by force was ignored. Elizabeth had given her official backing to Anjou's governorship of the Low Countries, and would not interfere with his military manoeuvres.

In July 1584, immediately after William's death, Herle, writing directly to the queen herself, counselled with still greater urgency that an English force ought to be sent, this time to hold the Prince of Parma's Spanish forces at Zutphen:

> If the enemy [the Prince of Parma, acting for Spain] may be entertained for these two months following from prevailing at Zutphen, (which considering his necessity and other difficulties that he is encumbered with, may well be hoped for) then assuredly, Right Gracious Sovereign, he is barred from all means and practices, that he has projected upon the Prince's death. And the States are assured till the next spring by reason of the waters that will be risen about Zutphen and elsewhere . . . And the states are to provide by God's grace of further remedy abroad and at home . . . only wanting a sufficient head of power and wealth to command them.

Eventually Zutphen did turn out to be an important town strategically for Protestant resistance to the Spanish after William's death.

The intelligencer, however, here overstepped the mark in his obvious enthusiasm to involve English troops in affairs in the Low Countries. This is one of the few occasions on which we have a record of Herle being reprimanded by his patron Leicester for going beyond his brief as a spy, by proposing policy (military intervention) rather than pure intelligence.[60] Herle was, in fact, more prescient than he knew in signalling the symbolic importance of outmanoeuvring Parma at Zutphen. The hero of English Protestantism, Sir Philip Sidney, would be fatally wounded there under Leicester's command in 1585, and it was the eventual loss of control of Zutphen and surrounding territories that finally sealed the failure of Leicester's Low Countries adventure at the end of 1587.

Among the many bizarre alleged plots against Queen Elizabeth's life uncovered by her assiduous secret service during the 1580s, two stand out for their close emotional association with the attempts on William of Orange's life (plots possibly closely contrived to cause alarm by the secret services themselves). The lurid accounts which were circulated in the Elizabethan equivalent of the tabloid press – detailing the way the plots unfolded, their eventual discovery, the testimony of informants and the arraignment and punishment of the would-be perpetrators – tell us a good deal about the atmosphere of anxiety and mistrust which followed the violent intrusions into William's household of Jauregay and Gérard. They also reveal how the pistol or 'dag' which was supposedly the weapon to be used in both these failed assassination attempts becomes a particular focus for generalised fear and unease, and an emblem for the widely-perceived threat of Spanish anti-Protestant violence finding its way into the very heart of English affairs.[61] In 1582, shortly after Jauregay's unsuccessful assassination attempt on William in March, 'one Mr. Somerville, or Somerfield, a Warwickshire gentleman, in the presence of witnesses declared that he meant to shoot the Queen with a dagg and hoped to see her head set on a pole, for she was a serpent and a viper'.[62] Somerville, who claimed he was acting alone, had let it be widely known that he would approach the queen without warning on horseback, while she was out riding at her leisure, and kill her with a pistol-shot.

The 'plot', if such it really was, clearly resembles that used successfully in the assassination of the Duke of Guise in France twenty years earlier. That violent pistol-murder had been carried out in the midst of the French civil wars, when an encounter with an armed horseman was a serious danger to be avoided (we might compare Montaigne's account of how, during the same period, he had recovered consciousness after a fall from his horse convinced he had been attacked by a rider with an arquebus). In heavily-policed London, with Catholics under constant surveillance, Somerville's plot seems far-fetched. 'The idea which he had conceived of going alone to London and shooting the Queen with a dagg hardly bears the marks of sanity. The public manner in which he boasted of his intentions tends to strengthen the supposition.'[63] Someone who had heard Somerville loudly announcing his intended deed notified the authorities. He was arrested, along with his priest and his father-in-law. The three were tried, condemned, and sentenced to be executed. Somerville never reached the scaffold, but was found hanged in his cell. He probably committed suicide, although one of Walsingham's spies reported that he had been done away with to stop him betraying his fellow-conspirators: 'Somerville was hanged to avoid a mischief.'[64]

The Parry plot of 1585, while its contours were filled out by interrogations and witness statements to indicate what was apparently a more substantial plan, is nevertheless similarly implausible as a serious attempt on the queen's life. A luridly detailed account was widely circulated following Parry's execution, carrying the sensational title:

> A True and plain declaration of the horrible Treasons, practised by William Parry the Traitor, against the Queen's Majesty. The manner of his Arraignment, Conviction and execution, together with the copies of sundry letters of his and others, tending to divers purposes, for the proofs of his Treason. Moreover, a few observations gathered of his own words and writings, for the further manifestations of his most disloyal, devilish and desperate purpose.

Plainly intended to whip up agitation against English Catholics and their supposed foreign masters (particularly Mary, Queen of Scots, incarcerated by the English but still considered a grave political liability), the pamphlet gives graphic detail of the plot, the evidence against Parry, his confession and a grisly account of his execution.

According to the pamphlet, Dr William Parry (the 'Dr' attached to his name probably suggested to contemporaries that he was dangerously overeducated) had 'long led a wasteful and dissolute life', which had culminated in his leaving England following his arrest on a charge of attempted murder over a disputed debt. During his travels, so went the broadsheet version, he converted to Catholicism, and 'upon conference with certain Jesuits and others of like quality' was recruited to attempt the queen's murder, 'which he bound himself by promise, letters, and vows, to perform and execute'.

In fact, while in Newgate gaol awaiting sentencing some time in 1580, Parry had been recruited by Elizabeth's secret service, released and sent to Europe to infiltrate the English Catholics there. As early as June 1580 he was sending reports about the movements of English Catholics in France to Burghley from Paris. In September 1582 he moved to Lyon. On 10 May 1583 he wrote from there to Burghley: 'If I am not deceived I have shaken the foundations of the English Seminary at Rheims and utterly overthrown the credit of the English pensioners at Rome.'[65]

In January 1584 Parry returned to England, and in March approached the queen, claiming that he had secret information, acquired on the Continent, which he was anxious to deliver to her in person. He managed to inveigle his way into her presence at Whitehall Palace, 'as her Majesty had but one only Counsellor with her at the time of his access, in a remote place, who was so far distant, as he could not hear his speech'.

Like Jauregay and Gérard, Parry apparently produced intelligence of sufficient sensitivity and importance that he gained the trust of both the queen and her immediate advisers. Crucially, it involved conversations he had had with Mary Stuart's agent in Paris, Thomas Morgan. Like Gérard he confessed to his sovereign to having acted as a double agent, but insisted that he had now resolved to serve only herself and the Protestant cause. In fact, so the tabloid version tells us, 'his only intent of discovering the same in sort as he craftily and traiterously did, tended to no other end, but to make the way the easier to accomplish his most devilish and wicked purpose'.

Parry was thereafter granted regular access to the queen, who grew increasingly to trust him, settling a 'most liberal' pension on him. He was also given a seat in the 1584 Parliament. There he once again attracted negative attention from the authorities with a passionate and disruptive speech against legislation being enacted to further restrict the rights of English Catholics which resulted in his being 'committed to the Sergeant's ward' by the order of the House.

It was after this, in February 1585, that, according to the broadsheet, Parry proposed a plot to assassinate the queen to Sir Edmund Neville, hoping perhaps to draw from Neville, who was strongly suspected of sympathy with the cause of Elizabeth's enemies, some treasonable answer.[66] The 'plot' he revealed to Neville, in other words, may have been no more than an *agent provocateur*'s attempt to encourage a potential security threat to reveal himself, in order to trap him. Neville, however, went straight to the authorities. Parry was arrested and interrogated. He confessed freely, without being subjected to torture (though it was threatened), and indeed wrote a letter admitting his heinous designs against her to the queen herself.

The lurid broadsheet account of Parry's treason is liberally embellished with details to make the plot plausible to a credulous public. It neatly rings all necessary bells to keep its English readers alarmed and compliant with a regime whose repressive measures and absence of civil liberties were supposedly a responsible reaction to ever-present threats all around them. Readers are alerted to the double-dealings of apparently loyal servants of the queen, they are made sceptical of the intentions of Members of Parliament who supported any legislative challenge to the status quo, and are urged to be dismayed by the wicked and treasonous goings-on among Catholics and Catholic sympathisers. Finally, they are encouraged to be deeply mistrustful of the intrigues and scheming associated with the presence in prison in England of Mary Stuart. Both Parry's own confession and Neville's colourful tale of the plot Parry revealed to him bring in the name of Thomas Morgan and the Scottish queen's supporters in Paris.

Meanwhile Elizabeth is represented in the tale as endlessly gracious, forgiving, generous and inclined to think the best of her subjects. It is she who insists that Parry be given a chance to explain himself to Leicester and Sir Christopher Hatton. Under interrogation by them, Parry supposedly recalls his conversation with Neville, and that it might have been construed as treasonous:

> And being lodged that night at Master Secretary's house, the next morning he desired earnestly to have some further speech with Master Secretary: which granted, Parry declared to him that he had called to remembrance that he had once some speech with one Neville a kinsman of his (so he called him) touching a point of doctrine contained in the answer made to the book, entitled, The Execution of Justice in England, by which book it was resolved, that it was lawful to take away the life of a prince, in furtherance of the Catholic religion: but he protested that they never had any speech at all of any attempt intended against her Majesty's person.[67]

Here, as in the case of the attempts against the life of the Prince of Orange, it is Catholic literature expressly urging true believers (and true servants of the Catholic sovereigns who had undertaken to defend the true faith) that they are entitled to kill 'infidel' rulers with impunity.

Neville was now produced, and repeated his claim that Parry had tried to lure him into a plot to assassinate the queen. Parry's response was that it was one man's word against the other – one agent's name against another's. Neville, however, 'did with great constancy affirm all that he had before said, and did set down many probable circumstances of the times, places, and of such other accidents as had happened between them in the course of that action: whereupon Parry was then committed to the Tower'. On the strength of Neville's detailed written evidence, and his own confessions, Parry was found guilty of treason. His execution was to be carried out at Westminster on 2 March 1585, according to the sentence recorded in the broadsheet:

Since thou hast been indicted of the treasons comprised in
the indictment, and thereupon arraigned, and hast confessed
thyself guilty of them, the Court doth award, that thou shalt
be had from hence to the place whence thou didst come,
and so drawn through the open city of London upon a
hurdle to the place of execution, and there to be hanged up
and let down alive, and thy privy parts cut off, and thy
entrails taken out and burnt in thy sight, then thy head to
be cut off, and thy body to be divided in four parts, and to
be disposed at her Majesty's pleasure: And God have mercy
on thy soul.

Execution for an act of treason was always intended to be enacted
as a dreadful lesson to those who so much as dreamed of an act
of violence against the sovereign – dreaming treason was itself, if
uttered, potentially prosecutable as a treasonous act. We will never
know whether Parry was actually a potential pistol-wielding
assassin, or merely a double agent who had fallen foul of those who
controlled him. But his execution performed for the Elizabethan
public the ghastly spectacle of the state, like his mangled body,
mutilated, tormented and torn into separate pieces, by Catholic-
inspired mischief-makers from overseas.

PSYCHOLOGICAL WARFARE

In the justifications given by the perpetrators of both the Somerville and the Parry plots, their insistence (like Jauregay and
Gérard) that the acts they intended to commit were sanctioned by
a higher authority figures prominently in the popular accounts.
Edward Neville, testifying to Parry's attempts to involve him in
his plot, records how Parry tried to persuade him that 'killing her

Majestie' was 'an Acte honourable, and meritorious to God and the world':

> Wherein, saith he, if you will go with me, I will lose my life, or deliver my Country from her bad and tyrannous government. At which speeches finding me discontented, he asked me if I had read Doctor Allen's book, out of which he alleged an authority for it. I answered, No, and that I did not believe that authority. Well said he, what will you say, if I show further authority than this, even from Rome itself, a plain dispensation for the killing of her, wherein you shall find it (as I said before) meritorious.

As in our own time the idea that the followers of one faith are convinced that suicide bombings and hostage executions are 'just' and sanctioned by divine authority causes consternation, so Europe's Protestants responded with horrified indignation to the idea that attempts on the lives of Protestant sovereigns could be promoted as just actions by Catholic authorities. Neville counters Parry's claim that Catholic teaching smiles on his attempt to assassinate Elizabeth by protesting that no rational argument can entitle the believer – however passionate for his faith – to think that a crime is acceptable because divinely sanctioned:

> Good cousin, said I, when you shall show it me, I shall think it very strange, when I shall see one to hold that for meritorious, which another holdeth for damnable.

Fear of impending violent calamity attached itself to the hidden death-delivering weapon which figured regularly in both failed and successful assassination plots. The fact that it was once again an assassin carrying a concealed pistol who carried out William's eventual murder in 1584 rapidly acquired strong symbolic significance in England. The handgun stood for the ever-present threat of Catholicism reaching into the heart of Protestant England to snatch the life of the monarch. At the same time, the handgun carried by stealth into the private quarters of the victim also symbolised the disturbing way in which totalitarian rulers could insinuate their power into the deepest, most personal recesses of their subjects' lives – compare the way in which the residents of Baghdad were initially reluctant to express relief at the toppling from power of Saddam Hussein, continuing to believe that he might take revenge on them in their own homes.

For those in positions of authority, William's assassination had repercussions that reached far beyond the Netherlands. The crowned heads of Europe – always fearful of attempts on their lives – reeled at the idea that their security was now threatened by a lethal weapon of hitherto unimagined effectiveness which could kill from a distance, and which could be carried concealed and undetected by the murderer into the presence of the unsuspecting victim.

It was noted that Gérard had twice been rebuffed by William's guards – once as William passed through the hallway on his way to dinner, and once as Gérard appeared to wish to present a paper to the prince as he left the meal. On both occasions the would-be assassin was prevented from approaching his victim closely enough to use the second weapon concealed in his clothing, a short dagger. Even so, the guards had been powerless to stop the determined assailant from eventually discharging his pistol from a distance of a few paces from the Dutch leader.

The spectre of the undetected assassin is a perennially potent one. Protestant pamphlet-writers obsessively revisited the circumstances under which Gérard, though twice identified as a potential threat, had nevertheless gained access to the Prince of Orange and successfully carried out his assassination. Their horrified disbelief prefigures the similar revisiting by journalists and official investigators of the 11 September 2001 attacks on the twin towers in New York – the unheeded intelligence warnings prior to the event, and the fact that several of the terrorists had been stopped by security at Boston airport (one of them twice), yet had been allowed to board the planes they subsequently crashed into the twin towers and the Pentagon. Such rehearsals of how disaster might have been averted betray the deep psychological damage inflicted on a nation by terrorist atrocities. At any moment, apparently, the individual with murderous intent and a deadly concealed weapon might penetrate even the most apparently secure location. His indifference to his own survival makes the most stringent of security checks useless to stop him – his cool submission to search (as shown on the video footage of the Al Qaida terrorists at Boston airport) throws the security guards off his track.

Death by pistol-shot from a concealed weapon was an ever-present fear for the princes of sixteenth-century Europe, just as the suicide attacker armed with explosives or toxic substances has become the nightmare globally for the twenty-first century. The murder of the Prince of Orange intensified the sense of something close to panic in England, over the possibility of a successful assassination attempt against the queen.

Yet in truth, the political situation in England barely resembled that in the Low Countries, or even in France. There was no state of civil war in England, and no ongoing rebellion against occupying forces – the conditions which lent themselves to desperate fanaticism, and infiltration of one party's camp by an alien insurgent, and thus to opportunities for sudden violence and targeted killing. In the end, we may conclude that the assassination of William of Orange conveniently allowed Elizabeth's security services in England, and those ministers who controlled them, to tighten their political stranglehold on the English population by fear, internal surveillance, sudden arrests and interrogations, all in the name of 'safety'. In fearful times, erosion of civil liberties which amounts to tyranny may be suffered resignedly, once it is dressed up as being in the interests of 'Homeland Security'.

6

English Aftermath 2 —
Pistols and Politics

REELING FROM THE CONSEQUENCES

IN AN INSTANT, the pistol shot that killed the Prince of Orange changed the course of European history. William's death brought England, which had been hesitating on the edge of Low Countries affairs for decades, undecided as to whether the Dutch were rebels or freedom fighters, for a short time into strategic prominence. With Spain and England finally in open confrontation, the assassination also led directly to Philip II's decision to launch the 'Invincible Armada' and attempt an English conquest in 1588. England's subsequent defeat of the Spanish Armada was taken as dramatic confirmation of her position as a major power on the world stage.

The immediate effect of the successful attempt on William's life in 1584 was shocked disbelief and political paralysis across Europe. His death dramatically weakened the position of the Protestant provinces in the Low Countries, threatening to fragment the precarious series of anti-Spanish alliances he had brokered and maintained through his personal powers of persuasion. The key provinces of Holland and Zeeland, which William the Silent had held together for ten years as a bulwark against Spain, again became vulnerable, thereby once more raising the spectre of a Spanish invasion of England herself. Were Philip now allowed to reconquer the Low Countries in their entirety, regaining Holland and Zeeland, the possibility of a Spanish fleet attacking unmolested, or even supported by a Dutch Catholic fleet joining the assault from the shelter of the north-western coast of the Netherlands, became a reality. Yet for months no foreign power was prepared to make a move to come to the assistance of the States of Holland.

Gradually, and with considerable reluctance, the Queen of England was persuaded fully to involve herself in the Dutch Revolt. It was, to begin with, at the personal level that Elizabeth was drawn into Low Countries business in the aftermath of the prince's assassination. William's widow and family were in desperate need of succour. Ten days after the prince's death, William Herle reported to Elizabeth I the state of total confusion at the Orange court and the pitiful state of his widow, Louise de Coligny. Herle's letter is unusual, coming as it does from a mere intelligence agent, in the directness with which it urges the queen to become involved. But then, the circumstances were exceptional, even for a spy:

> I visited the Princess of Orange by her own request, whom I found in a most dark little melancholic chamber, which was a twice sorrowful sight to behold her heaviness and apparel [state of dress], augmented by the dolefulness of the place. And truly the perplexity was great that I found her in, not only for the consideration of things past, but for that which might follow hereafter; her afflictions having been great. She [and her daughters] all with a most tender affection recommended their service unto your Majesty, as to a Lady of all ladies, but especially the two Princesses in most humble and wise sort, expressed a certain fervent devotion towards your Majesty.[68]

In fact, by the time Elizabeth received this letter she had already written expressing her condolences and shock to the Princess of Orange. She was clearly deeply upset by the sudden violent death of a head of state with whose interests she was temperamentally in sympathy, and whose political situation in many ways so closely resembled her own. Aside from the gravity of the political situation created by William's murder, she recognised the vulnerability of her own position in his violent end. In her letter she expressed her grief at hearing the sad news of the death of the prince and her sympathy with the princess for her great loss, 'hoping that she will bear it with Christian resignation':

> If nature could give place to reason, so that she might think rather of his good than of her own loss, who by his last words, recommending himself to God with the poor afflicted people of those countries, manifested to the world his Christian determination to carry on the cause which he had embraced; then she would have no less occasion to rejoice at the happy issue of his life (contrary to the calumnious reports of his enemies) than the authors of this execrable act have had reason to wish that they had never been born, whose more than barbarous malice will endure, to their infamy, for all time.[69]

Elizabeth's personal shock is clear from her tone. On the matter of money to support the widow, her infant son and her many stepchildren, she was, however, characteristically vague:

> Touching the Princess's own affairs, considering the warm affection which her Majesty bore to the late Prince, and the devotion which those of her Excellency's house have always shown to her, and which will ever dwell in her memory, she will never fail to do her all the good offices she can.

Louise de Coligny, the Princess of Orange and daughter herself of a great military man, did not in the end rely on the vain hope that the notoriously parsimonious Elizabeth would look after her orphaned children. She took practical steps too: she wrote to Sir John Norris, whose forces had stoutly defended the cause of her dead husband, asking him to accept her stepson Maurice as a soldier volunteer.[70]

Slowly, over the months following William's death, Elizabeth allowed herself to be persuaded that the only acceptable solution to the political crisis it had caused was to send English troops to help the beleaguered and leaderless Dutch Protestants. To make it clear that she did so under pressure of circumstances and still against her better judgement, she issued a strong public declaration in September 1585: 'Declaration of the causes moving the queen to give aid to the ... low countries'. Like Philip II's Ban and William of Orange's 'Apology' earlier, Elizabeth's printed 'Declaration' was translated into at least five European languages and widely circulated for propaganda purposes. In it the queen insisted that it was through no ambition of her own for power in the Low Countries that she was prepared to intervene, but for the good of the Dutch people alone:

> The causes moving the queen to give aid to the defence of the people afflicted and oppressed in the Low Countries, were not any desire of aggrandizing either herself or her subjects, but to aid the natural people of those countries to defend their towns from sacking and desolation, and thereby to procure them safety, to the honour of God, whom they desire to serve sincerely as Christian people, according to his word, and to enjoy their ancient liberties; to free herself from invading neighbours; and to ensure a continuance of the old-standing intercourse of friendship and merchandise between her people and the inhabitants of those countries.[71]

The desire to 'ensure a continuance of the old-standing intercourse of friendship and merchandise' was high on Elizabeth's agenda. In August, while a Dutch embassy waited anxiously in London and she procrastinated, the great international port of Antwerp (under siege since the previous year) had fallen to the Spanish, terminating lucrative Anglo–Dutch trade there. The victorious Duke of Parma garrisoned the town with crack Spanish troops and issued an order that Protestants who refused to convert to Catholicism must leave. Over the next four years around half Antwerp's population, some thirty-eight thousand people, migrated north and Antwerp ceased to be the hub of Anglo–Dutch commercial business.[72]

FURTHERING ENGLISH INTERESTS

William the Silent had been involved in secret negotiations with both the future Duke of Anjou (the then Duke of Alençon) in France, and Elizabeth I as early as 1573, offering inducements in the form of revenues and political power if either would consent to become titular head of an independent Low Countries, and provide significant forces and revenue to drive Philip from the whole Netherlands.[73]

In 1573 William Herle wrote a meticulous account for Lord Burghley detailing confidential discussions he had had on behalf of English interests with Prince William concerning possible terms for official involvement in the Dutch conflict. He reported William's clear assessment of the danger Spanish conquest of the seaboard provinces of Holland and Zeeland would pose for England, and William's careful opinion of the kind of justification the queen might use for intervening in the conflict there without provoking out-and-out war with Spain. He stressed the dreadful consequences of England's inaction, and the precarious state of his own situation. Finally, he made his offer of terms to Elizabeth:

> [If she were] to acknowledge their offer and set foot in Holland she should presently have Flushing, Brill, Rotterdam, Enkhuisen in possession with what other places she would desire. They also would yearly contribute unto her the sum of 8 or 900,000 [crowns], and all her charges should not rise to 400,000 which would be given without grudge of any, or difficulty in the gathering of it: for then their traffic by sea and their husbandry at home should to their great benefit and by her Majesty's only means flourish and be well able to yield a greater reckoning than this.

To make his offer yet more tempting, Herle reported, Prince William had particularly emphasised the further tactical and commercial benefits which would flow almost immediately from her decision officially to enter the Netherlands conflict. Were she to accept his generous offer, he continued, she could count on bringing all the northern provinces over to her side in the conflict, and thereby acquire important commercial bases for Anglo–Dutch trade:

> In effect her Majesty should have there and in Zeeland, 32 great walled towns, both newly fortified and planted with garrison (for they have maintained by land and sea this whole year 34,000 persons, Pioneers, Mariners, and Soldiers and have at this instant above 200 ships in service) and withall she should be Mistress of the puissantest [most powerful] Navy in Christendom and of the aptest havens for the entertainment of them and of her own traffic with all nations, whereby if she would restore this again, in the end she might make . . . the honorablest composition and the profitablest that ever Prince made.[74]

Herle's setting out of the issues here is unusually clear and to the point – on the whole his reports tend to be verbose and disorganised. In 1586, at the end of a long letter to Walsingham, Leicester apologised for the fact that his letter 'is so long I cannot peruse it', and added: 'I am afraid you will compare me shortly to William Herle.'[75] But the eloquent arguments Herle relayed to the queen were to no avail. She still at this point refused to become embroiled in the Dutch Revolt, though she did agree covertly to help finance English forces under the 'independent' command of Sir John Norris. Although Anjou was somewhat more encouraging, he too at this stage hesitated to get involved, and the French also remained for the time being on the sidelines.

In January 1576 Prince William made another attempt. This time he sent his most trusted adviser Marnix to London to offer the English queen full sovereignty, over and above the terms previously proposed. By now, however, she was well aware that rejection of this offer was likely to lead to the same proposal being made next to Anjou and the French. Walsingham, who had been appointed secretary of state in May 1575, and who was strongly in favour of English military intervention, covertly advised Marnix and his Dutch delegation to play up the likelihood of French involvement when trying to secure Elizabeth's agreement to accepting titular sovereignty of the Protestant provinces. He told the envoys in confidence that Prince William would have to make it appear to Queen Elizabeth as if he were on the point of signing an agreement with the French king, because the queen would not be willing to give aid to the Dutch rebels until she was convinced that if she did not, the chief ports of the Netherlands would fall into French hands.[76] Nevertheless, unwilling to provoke direct confrontation with Spain, and thereby to enter into open-ended commitments of soldiers and expenditure, Elizabeth turned William down.

When, as feared, it looked as though William would immediately call on Anjou instead, the queen launched a hasty diplomatic counter-offensive. Walsingham was sent to talk to the States General, to try to agree to a commitment short of money and men which would stop William's approaching the French. Exceeding his brief as usual, Walsingham reassured William that troops would be forthcoming. At the same time he wrote to London asking for agreement that if 'necessity shall induce her Majesty to send forces, my Lord of Leicester will come over without delay'.[77]

On 7 March 1577 the Earl of Leicester wrote to William telling him that the prince had never stood so high in the queen's estimation, and William responded with a typical flourish. When his third wife Charlotte of Bourbon gave birth to a daughter on 26 March, William named her Elizabeth, and invited the Earl of Leicester to stand as godfather. Sir Philip Sidney, who was already on the Continent on government business, was diverted from his return route to attend the christening on his uncle Leicester's behalf. William and Sidney took to one another immediately, and the visit established Sidney as an influential figure in Anglo–Dutch Protestant affairs.

Once again, William contrived a gesture of personal intimacy designed to seduce England into coming to his assistance. He chose this moment to summon his eldest daughter Maria to join him from the family estates in Germany. A rumour spread rapidly that William was going to offer Maria's hand in marriage to Sidney – Leicester's beloved nephew and the bright young hope of European Protestantism – thereby cementing Orange connections to the English Protestant nobility and (he hoped) hugely flattering Sidney's uncle Leicester.[78] Typically, however, William was hedging his bets: the States General believed that Maria was to be married to the son of a leading Dutch nobleman and competitor for power in the States of Holland, the Duke of Aerschot, to cement internal Low Countries alliances.[79] In the end she married neither.

In spite of such canny manoeuvring on both sides, it was the French whom the States of Holland finally succeeded in drawing into action in the Low Countries.[80] Concrete help from a French Catholic like Anjou, with a taste for military action, seemed a better prospect than endless procrastinating with an English Protestant queen. And in June 1584, although Anjou's 'French Fury' at Antwerp had definitively turned the Dutch people against the French, following Anjou's death and William's assassination in July it was still to the French that the States of Holland first turned for help. Only when the French king turned them down yet again did they appeal once more to Elizabeth as a last resort.

The pattern of William the Silent's wooing of first one and then the other of the Duke of Anjou and Queen Elizabeth on behalf of the Dutch Protestant cause is mirrored by the ageing Elizabeth's on-off encouragement of the belief that she might yet decide to marry the Duke of Anjou – a man twenty years her junior, a Frenchman and a Catholic to boot. However unpopular with the English people such a marriage would have been, it would have had the immediate effect of joining French and English interests in the Low Countries. After de la Noue's discovery of the Spanish plot to depose her once full conquest of the Low Countries had been achieved, Elizabeth became reconciled to backing Anjou in his challenge to Spain. In 1579, she let it be known that a marriage between herself and Anjou was once more a serious possibility, thereby raising the possibility of a marital Anglo–French alliance against Philip II.[81]

As soon as it was public knowledge that Anjou had accepted Dutch sovereignty in January 1581, Elizabeth once again launched a charm offensive against Anjou. She made elaborate professions of her love for the duke, summoning him to her side. In November she placed a ring on his finger and publicly announced her intention of going ahead with the marriage. While the Dutch waited for their new ruler to arrive, he lingered in England, enjoying the queen's lavish hospitality and her exaggerated professions of devotion.

When Anjou finally set off for the Low Countries in February 1582, Elizabeth insisted that he should be escorted by such a train of English noblemen, as was 'meet for his greatness'. He therefore arrived at Flushing to take up his new role with both the Earl of Leicester and Sir Philip Sidney in attendance. The English delegation were prominent in all the subsequent lavish entertainment laid on by William, their presence appearing to validate Anjou's appointment. When Anjou entered Antwerp as Duke of Brabant, to a royal welcome, Leicester rode directly in front of him alongside William of Orange. The magnificent large-format printed book recording in images and text the Duke of Anjou's 'joyous entry' into Antwerp was dedicated to Leicester, and a special presentation copy dispatched to him by William's chaplain Loyseleur de Villiers. Leicester had only recently returned to England when Jauregay made his attempt on William's life in March. Elizabeth finally broke off marriage negotiations with Anjou after he had attempted his second, more aggressive entry into Antwerp, by force a year later (the occasion of the infamous 'French Fury'). Not even for strategic reasons could a Queen of England countenance marriage to a man who had carried out an unprovoked attack on Dutch Protestants.

'THE END OF ALL OUR AMBITIONS'

By the time the Earl of Leicester was at last allowed by Queen Elizabeth to leave for the Low Countries, in December 1585, he had been hoping to lead an English initiative to rescue the Dutch Protestants for ten years. He had even raised troops before (in 1577–78), only to have to stand them down when the initiative as usual came to nothing through Elizabeth's equivocating. A vain, impatient man no longer in his prime, with a bad temper, who had little experience of military leadership, Leicester regarded himself as the chosen champion of the reformed religion in the Low Countries, and as a man with the charisma and intelligence to be able to unite the competing factions there as William the Silent had once done. By leading the English army into Holland, he believed, he was discharging his duty towards 'that noble man that is gone'.

For many English Protestants, intervention in the Low Countries was nothing less than a national crusade. All around them, the forces of Catholicism seemed to be mustering in a great international conspiracy to destroy them. Philip of Spain considered the religion of the English to be 'worse than either Turks, Marranos, Jews or infidels', according to that intrepid compiler of intelligence William Herle.[82] The pious offered prayers for Leicester's success, as another Joshua: 'the prayers of all the godly in the land, being touched with an inward sympathy and fellow feeling of their neighbour's calamities', as one English Puritan wrote in 1585, dedicating his work to Leicester.[83] Beyond this, to Leicester and Walsingham the Low Countries was the crucial test-case for the idea of a broader international Protestant cause – an alliance of the Protestant communities of northern Europe against the forces of Spain and the Counter-Reformation. No wonder the 'flower of English youth' – the bright young Protestant men of the English nobility, like Essex and Sidney, eagerly joined Leicester's train, and vied with one another to serve in his army.[84] Leicester landed at Flushing just after midday on Friday, 20 December 1585, and immediately a tide of Dutch euphoria swept over him. As he had anticipated, a great deal was expected of him on that side of the 'Narrow Sea' also. A senior Dutch figure had written to Walsingham shortly before his arrival:

> I doubt not but that God will bless all [the queen's] heroic enterprises, since she in a way brings back to life the late Prince of Orange in the person of the Earl of Leicester, on whose coming men have fixed their hopes that the affairs both of state and war will be restored to their ancient luster and splendour.[85]

At The Hague, Leicester was welcomed and entertained by William's son Maurice, the new stadholder and commander of the Dutch armed forces, who had been hastily elected in anticipation of the English arrival (prudently making sure that the Dutch had their own leader in post to counterbalance their new English one). Sir Philip Sidney acted as Leicester's guide and facilitator, smoothing relations between his uncle and his Low Countries hosts. In the evening there were fireworks and (as a member of Leicester's party reported) the 'making of bonfires after their manner, which is to fire great pitch barrels on the tops of high poles'. As Leicester and his train moved from town to town on what amounted to a royal progress, the citizens of each vied with one another as to how lavish and spectacular a display of welcome they could put on for the man they confidently assumed was to be their new governor general.

The fireworks display that marked the Earl of Leicester's entry into
The Hague in 1585

The continuing mood of excitement and expectation went to
Leicester's head. In January 1586, when the triumphant cavalcade
reached the University of Leiden – founded in 1575, and symbol
of William the Silent's hopes for a moderate, intellectual Protestantism – he allowed himself to be appointed governor general.
He knew that he had been expressly forbidden by the queen
herself to accept any Dutch title which might imply English rule
in the Low Countries. But, as he wrote to Burghley, it had been
almost impossible to refuse. The chancellor of Leiden University
had, he reported, delivered a long discourse in French 'of her
Majesty's goodness, of the love of the country to her, of the trust
they had in her above all the world, of the necessity they had for
safety of their state and countries':

> And as there was no prince in the world whom they owed
> obedience and duty unto, but to her Majesty, so seeing the
> credit and trust it pleased her to put me in here already, and
> the favour, credit, and I cannot tell what, so many good
> words they used of me, they took knowledge of that I had

> long had at her Majesty's hands . . . and therefore with one
> whole consent they did there beseech me, . . . that I would
> take the place and name of absolute governor and general of
> all their forces and soldiers, with their whole revenues, taxes,
> compositions, and all manner of benefits that they have, or
> may have, to be put freely and absolutely into my hands.[86]

'The queen of England,' he went on, 'they would serve as their
mistress, and under me as her minister here, with a better will
than ever they served under the prince of Orange; yet they loved
him well, but they never hoped of the liberty of this country till
now.'

It made not a bit of difference: Elizabeth was furious, not least
because she believed Burghley and her ministers had contrived
to keep the news of Leicester's acceptance of implied English
sovereignty in the Netherlands from her for weeks. No matter
how often Leicester tried to explain in his letters how much she
stood to gain (particularly the financial advantages), the queen's
anger was undiminished. As Leicester moved from the 'triumphs'
of greeting into the military campaign proper, she bombarded the
States General with indignant letters denying that she had agreed
to have him 'reign' in the Low Countries in her stead. She thereby
further undermined Leicester's increasingly difficult position.

For the military campaign began badly and got worse. There
were disagreements from the outset between Leicester and Norris
as to how the campaign was to be run (and indeed, over who was
in charge). Young men like Essex were impatient to fight in earnest, and frustrated by all the waiting around. Engagements were
minor and their outcomes indecisive; they consisted largely in
harrying Spanish forces, and taking over more or less reluctant
small towns. Under the Duke of Parma, the Spanish army was
steadily consolidating its hold over towns and territory previously

lost to William the Silent. It was not clear how the English-led army of liberation was going to bring about the much-looked-for decisive victory.

A pitched battle finally took place at the end of September 1586, outside Zutphen. Leicester's troops had encircled the town, hoping to draw Parma into battle when he attempted to resupply it. On 22 September, Parma took the bait. Tipped off the previous evening by a Spanish deserter, Leicester sent Sir John Norris to intercept the supply convoy. Although this was Leicester's chance for a major engagement, he assigned Norris only three hundred cavalry and two hundred foot-soldiers.[87]

Leading the English cavalry charge which was supposed to take the Spanish by surprise was a troop of fifty light horsemen, armed with several pistols apiece, and wearing lightweight armour (and no leg armour) for speed and manoeuvrability in the field. These pistoleers were the men with good, fast horses, and the latest in technical equipment (wheel-lock pistols). They included the cream of English fighting men and most of the young noblemen from the Earl of Leicester's train: the Earl of Essex, Peregrine Lord Willoughby, Sir Philip Sidney, Sir William Knollys, Sir Philip Butler, Sir Henry Unton, Sir Robert Sidney and Sir Roger Williams. The last five of these were knighted *in situ* after the battle for their gallantry. Essex was given the senior title of knight banneret.

The engagement began at dawn, in dense fog. As this burned off, it was revealed that the Spanish troops far outnumbered their ambushers, and were well dug in in anticipation of attack. The best the English could achieve was the inflicting of some significant damage on the front row of Spanish pikemen (in that first light horse skirmish), further damage caused by Norris's men backing them up, and finally an orderly withdrawal. Philip Sidney was wounded in the thigh, though at first his wound was not believed to be life-threatening.

Sidney's death on 17 October was a bitter blow for his uncle Leicester (who by 1586 was hoping Sidney might succeed him as English commander in the Low Countries), and a symbolic disaster for the English Protestant 'crusade'. By his death after Zutphen, Sidney was elevated to the status of Protestant martyr – cut down in his prime, battling against the tyranny of Spanish Catholicism. The posthumous cult of Sir Philip Sidney matched that in our own time for Diana, Princess of Wales: a contemporary described it as 'a conquest of death by fame in his life'. Leicester, personally devastated (he had sent almost daily letters of reassurance to Sidney's father-in-law Walsingham, assuring him he would recover), arranged for his body to be carried back to England with full ceremony, on a boat with black sails. There Sidney was given a state funeral, his coffin escorted through the streets of London by a cortège of seven hundred mourners, including Sir Francis Drake and the Earls of Leicester, Huntingdon, Pembroke and Essex.

Leicester came back to England from the Low Countries in late November 1586, leaving Sir John Norris in charge of his English troops on the ground. In August, Walsingham had uncovered another plot (the Babington Plot) to assassinate Elizabeth and put her Catholic cousin Mary Stuart (Mary, Queen of Scots) on the throne, raising fears of an imminent Spanish invasion. William the Silent's death greatly heightened such fears, and faced with what seemed like incontrovertible evidence of the Scottish queen's involvement in plots against her life, Elizabeth was now finally persuaded to sign Mary's death warrant. Although Elizabeth claimed subsequently to have rescinded her consent, Mary's execution took place on 8 February 1587.

Leicester returned briefly to the Low Countries that summer

with three thousand fresh troops. By now, however, hopes that the arrival of the English would bring about a Protestant salvation had all but evaporated, and Dutch support for the earl was decidedly lukewarm. After a failed attempt to stamp his authority on The Hague (and possibly to arrest William's son, Maurice of Nassau), Leicester abandoned his hopes of personal fame and fortune in the Netherlands, and returned to England for good in December 1587. He relinquished his command 'with a mixture of relief and bitterness, his hopes of being another William of Orange completely shattered'.[88]

In summer 1588, the Spanish launched their Invincible Armada, with the aim of conquering England. Intelligence of the impending attack had been received in England during the preceding months, and the Earl of Leicester helped organise defences on the south coast. In the event these defences were never tested. As the formidable Spanish fleet bore down on England, its commander, the Duke of Medina Sidonia, ordered it to pause off the Dutch coast at Gravelines, hoping for further reinforcements. On 7 August, Sir Francis Drake attacked with a small English fleet, while the Spanish ships were out of formation. The damage he inflicted was psychological rather than material – in fact only a single Spanish ship was sunk. The Armada regrouped and sailed on, virtually intact, only to be vanquished by the forces of nature as Medina Sidonia, his plans thwarted by contrary winds, attempted to sail home round the coast of Ireland, rather than attempt to retrace his outward journey and encounter further English naval resistance. As the Spanish fleet rounded the northern coast of Scotland between 11 and 24 September on its way home it was struck by appalling weather and driven back on to the coast of Ireland. At least twenty-one ships were wrecked on the Scottish and Irish rocks. England thus owed the defeat of the Invincible Armada as much to the extreme weather as to her own planning and military prowess. Nevertheless, the impact across Europe of the victory of the English navy over the assembled naval might of Spain was symbolically of enormous and lasting importance.

In early September 1588, Robert Dudley, Earl of Leicester, died at his country house in Oxfordshire after a brief bout of fever. He was aged fifty-five or fifty-six, and had been travelling in the countryside to recuperate from the rigours of the Armada campaign.[89] Gabriel Harvey, close friend of the poet Edmund Spenser, who like so many others had belonged to Leicester's extensive intellectual and intelligence entourage, saw this as the end of all the hopes of the Protestant war party in England. He wrote in the margin of his copy of Frontinus's *Stratagems* [of war]: '1588. *Revolutio meae Reformationis, seu Annus Assuetudinis*' – '1588. The end of all our ambitions, or the year of my accustoming myself to my lot'.[90]

Leicester's failure finally put paid to Dutch hopes of salvation from overseas, and helped establish the line of the house of Orange as dynastic democratic rulers in the Low Countries. After his departure, the eighteen-year-old Maurice of Nassau officially took up William the Silent's position as stadholder and commander. When Maurice died without an heir in 1625, his half-brother Frederick Henry, son of Louise de Coligny, who had been a babe in arms when his father was assassinated, became the next stadholder. It was the marriage of Frederick Henry's fourteen-year-old son to Charles I's twelve-year-old daughter Mary in 1642, creating an Anglo–Dutch dynastic alliance, which eventually allowed the English to call upon the son of that union, William III of Orange (who in his turn had married a Mary Stuart, Charles II's niece), to drive the Catholic James II out of England and in 1689 claim the English throne.

Finale

A bullet from the back of a bush
Took Medgar Evers' blood.
A finger fired the trigger to his name.
A handle hid out in the dark
A hand set the spark
Two eyes took the aim
Behind a man's brain
But he can't be blamed
He's only a pawn in their game.

Bob Dylan, 'Only a Pawn in their Game' (1963)[91]

THE UNEXPECTED FIRING of a pistol still causes shock and panic today. Even if the sound of the shot is not unexpected, it nevertheless has an extraordinary impact. The sound of a pistol, fired by the starter on the running track, is still relied on to galvanise the runners into immediate action.

Even if the pistol is a toy one, most people feel nervous looking down its barrel. Once, while I was sipping coffee with a friend in a café in Cambridge, a small child across the room pointed his six-shooter in the direction of a man at the table adjacent to ours and shouted 'Bang!' The man obediently toppled from his chair and fell to the floor, causing absolute consternation, particularly to the little boy (several tables away, and quite unknown to him) who had pulled the trigger. The child's make-believe appeared to have turned suddenly serious. Replica guns make successful weapons in robberies because no one who finds a gun pointed directly at them wants to discover whether the pulling of the trigger will or will not result in a real bullet being fired.

Even when the celebrity victim is not politically powerful, one pistol shot can have a profound effect. John Lennon's killing in the street outside his apartment in New York, by a pistol-wielding fan who hours earlier had asked him for his autograph, has remained lastingly in the public imagination. It permanently altered the relationship between celebrities and their fans, destroying the bond of trust between them. Sometimes handgun assassinations have made large-scale reputations for little-known figures in the entertainment industry – that uncanny kind of glamour associated with the handgun raises an inconsequential violent death above the banal. How many of the general public had heard of the rap singer Tupac Shakur before he was gunned down in Las Vegas as part of a gangland feud?

Most people imagine that handguns and the mayhem they can cause in a moment in the hands of an assassin are a relatively new phenomenon. As we have seen, that is not the case. Pistols have been used with intent to kill, to alter events decisively, since the sixteenth century. In 1584 in Delft in the Low Countries, three bullets fired by a rogue assassin with a new-fangled wheel-lock pistol cut down the Prince of Orange, and in an instant altered the course of European history.

APPENDICES

NOTES

BIBLIOGRAPHY

INDEX

APPENDIX 1

*A Proclamation and an Edict in the form of a Proscription,
made by the Majesty of the King our Lord, against William of
Nassau, Prince of Orange, at the chief Captain and disturber
of the state of Christendom, and specially of these Low
Countries, by which every one is authorised, to hurt him and
to kill him, as a public plague, with a reward to him that
shall do it, and shall be assisting and aiding thereunto*

Philip by the grace of God King of Castile, of Leon, of Arragon, of
Navarre, of Naples, of Sicilia, of Maleorcha, of Sardinia, of the Isles, of
the Indies and the firm land, of the Ocean Sea, Archduke of Austria,
Duke of Burgundy, of Lothier, of Brabant, of Lembourg, of Luxem-
bourg, of Gelderland, and of Milan, Count of Habsburg, of Flanders,
of Artois, of Burgundy, Palatine both of Hainault, of Holland, of Zeeland, of Namur, and of Zutphen, Prince of Swave, Marquis of the holy
Empire, Lord of Friseland, of Salines, of Malines, of the City, Towns
and country of Utrecht, of Overyssel, and Groningen, and Governor
in Asia and Africa. To all those that shall see these present writings,
greeting.

It is known to all the world, how the late Emperor of most excellent
memory, Charles the first [fifth], my Lord and father, whom God
absolve, hath favourably handled and dealt with William of Nassau,
for the succession of the late René of Challon, Prince of Orange his
cousin: and how from that time forward, even from his first age, he
hath (although he were a stranger [foreigner]) greatly advanced him,
which thing we ourselves also, have always successively continued, and
dayly augmented more and more, having made him first of our order,
afterward our Lieutenaunt general in the government of Holland, Zeeland, Utrecht and of Burgundy, and withal, of our counsel of estate,
bestowing upon him sundry benefits and honours, whereby both by
reason of the other of fidelity and homages, which he hath likewise

made unto us, because also of the fees, pensions, lands and Lordships, held of us in divers our Countries and Provinces, he was greatly subjected and bound to obey us, to keep and hold his faith given, and to procure the good and profit of our affairs, and consequently to maintain, all quietness and peace in our estates and countries.

Notwithstanding every one knoweth, that we were not so soon departed, out of those our Low Countries, but that the said William of Nassau, made Prince of Orange by the means above mentioned, did by his sinister practises, devises and crafts assay [try], first, to get the good wills of those whome he knew to be discontent, greatly indebted, haters of justice, studious of novelties, and specially such as were suspected to be of the religion banqueting them, provoking them, and drawing them after him, by fair words, promises, and vain persuasions, even so far, that he was the principal authour, promotor, and framer, of the first request, presented by certain companies of young Gentlemen, who did daily frequent his house and table: yea that the very plot thereof, was laid in his said house, by and with the assistance of Count Ludovick of Nassau his brother a great heretic.

And albeit, that he was the director of all these devises, yet in that time, he daily haunted the counsel of estate, being present at all consultations and resolutions, taken and made therein, in so much that every man may easily mark, the faithful trust that was in him, and the observation of his oaths. And afterward passing from the said request, and proceeding further, he and his adherents, brought in heretical preachings, and public assemblies in sundry places of our said countries, while that the Duchess of Parma, our most dear and beloved sister (then Regentess and general Governess of our said Low Countries) had sent unto us, that we might give order concerning the said request. And also, by the advise, knowledge, and partaking of the said Prince of Orange the heretics (being guided by those presenters of the aforesaid request, who were favoured by him) began tumultuously to break Images, Alters, and Churches, to prophane all holy and sacred things, yea the sacraments instituted by god . . .

On the other side it is manifest, what we have continually done, to pacify and quiet (as soon as we understood thereof) the evil that fell out, as hath been said, between our said Lieuetenaunt general, and the estates. But all the good that we have done, or our said brother, hath been suppressed and hid, in stead whereof the said Orange and his partakers, have devised a thousand slanders, the more to abuse our said subjects . . .

Notwithstanding the said Orange, fearing the reconciliation of our subjects with us, came so far, that he laid again new devises, not only for to hinder that matter, but also to make (if he could) for ever, the thing past hope of recovery, and altogether remediless, by going about to corrupt all with heresy, whereunto he attained in divers places, both by crafts, mischiefs, and perjuries, well known to him and all heretics, and also by mere force, using the same that he had practised before, to waste and destroy the provinces of Holland and Zeeland, casting all into the fire of popular tumult . . .

And generally, he hath so behaved himself in all manner of tyranny, that he hath driven from thence and rooted out all the people of the church, yea he hath so handled the Lords, and the whole principal Nobility of our countries that they have been enforced to withdraw themselves and to forsake their countries, to the end that he may reign and rule there, most absolutely, amongst the furies and tumults of the people the good being chased away . . .

For these causes which are so just, reasonable and lawful, using in this behalf the authority that we have over him, as well by virtue of the oaths of fidelity and obedience, which he hath sundry times taken unto us, as also being the absolute and sovereign Prince of the said Low Countries, for all his perverse and wicked deeds, and because he alone hath been the head, authour and promoter of these troubles, and the principal disturber of our whole estate: to be short, because he hath been the public plague of Christendom, we publish him for a traitor, and a wicked man, the enemy of us and of our countries, and as such a one have proscribed him, and do perpetually and for ever proscribe him, out of the said countries, all other our Estates, Kingdoms and Seignuries, interdicting and forbidding all our subjects, of what estate, condition or quality soever they be, not to haunt, live, be conversant, speak or communicate with him, openly or secretly, nor to receive him or lodge him in their houses, not to minister unto him meat, drink, fire, nor any other necessaries, in any sort whatsoever, upon pain to incur our indignation and displeasure, as hereafter shall be said.

And so we permit all, whether they be our subjects or others, for the execution of our said declaration and edict, to stay him, let him, and safely to keep his person, and to hurt him both in his goods, and also in his person and life, giving the said William of Nassau over unto all men, as the enemie of mankinde, graunting unto every one, all his goods moveable and unmoveable, that can take, occupy, or conquer the same, wheresoever they be, except those goods, which are at this present, in our power and possession.

And to the end indeed, that this matter may be the more effectually and readily performed, and so by that means our said people the sooner delivered, from this tyranny and oppression, we willing to reward virtue, and to punish vice, do promise in the word of a king, and as the minister of God, that if there be any found, either among our own subjects, or amongst strangers, so noble of courage, and desirous of our service, and the public good, that knoweth any means how to execute our said Decree, and to set us and himself free, from the aforesaid plague, delivering him unto us quick or dead, or at the least taking his life from him, we will cause, to be given and provided, for him and his heirs, in good land or ready money, choose him whether, immediately after the thing shall be accomplished, the sum of 25 thousand crowns of gold, and if he have committed any offence or fault, how great and grievous soever it be, we promise to pardon him the same, and from henceforth do pardon it, yea and if he were not before noble, we do make him noble, for his courage and valliant act: and if the principal doer, take with him for his aid, in the acomplishment of this enterprise, or execution of this his fact, other persons beside himself, we will bestow upon them benefits and a reward, and will give every one of them, according to their degree, and according to that service which they shall yield unto us in this behalf: pardoning them also whatsoever they have ill done, and making them likewise noble . . .

And nevertheless, seeing that at this present the said publications cannot be made, in the towns, countries and territories, occupied by the rebellion of the said Orange, we will that the publications which shall be made, in towns nearest thereunto, being under our obeisance, shall be wholly and all together of such force and effect, as if they had been utterly done in the circuits and places accustomed, and for such we have authorised, and by these presents doe authorise them, yea we will and command, that immediately they be printed in two sundry languages, by the sworn printers of our Universities of Louvain or Douai, to the end that it may more easily come, to all men's knowledge, and this is our pleasure, appointment, and good will. In witness whereof we have caused our great seal to be put to these presents, which were made in our town of Maastricht the 15 day of the month of March, and in the year of grace 1580 and of our kingdoms.[92]

APPENDIX 2

A copy of the Letters which my Lord the Prince of Orange,
sent unto the Kings and Potentates of Christendom

Sir, I doubt not, but that your Majesty hath been advertised of a certain Proscription which the King of Spain, hath appointed to be published against me, because he hath caused the same to be spread abroad in all languages, and hath sent it also into divers quarters of christendom. I and all my very good friends have thought, that I could not sufficiently defend mine honour (which I am advised and purposed not to hazard or indanger for any thing) but by setting a just defence, against this unjust Proscription. In regard whereof, I have presented unto my Lords, the estates of these countries, my answer: which answer also (for the maintenance of mine honour and reputation amongst the Princes and Potentates of Europe, who in respect of their preeminences and dignities, are the succours of poor Princes and distressed noble men) I have been bold to send unto them, and to you (Sir) particularly, most humbly beseeching your Majesty, that after you have seen it, you would yield like judgement thereof, as it hath pleased my Lords the Estates, who have been most faithfull witnesses of all mine actions, to do, and to esteem and iudge thereof also (as it shall please your Majesty to take knowledge of it) by their advise and counsel, which also is annexed to my said defence.

And because (Sir) your Majesty may think it strange, that the King of Spain, having heretofore violently taken from me all my goods, after that I had put my governements into the hands of the Duchess of Parma, then the Governesse of this estate, and had withdrawn my self into the country of Germany, the place of my nativity, where I kept myself peaceably among my brethren, kinsfolks and friends, as also I had fully purposed so to continue: and that, having at the same time, conveyed or carried away from the schools, my son the Count of Bueren, and both contrary to the privileges of the country, and against his own oath causing him to be carried prisoner into Spain, where he is as yet cruelly kept captive: and besides, having procured me to be condemned to death, by the Duke of Alva his own officer: because (I say) your Majesty may thinke it strange; that for all these reasons (which were neverthelesse very great and weighty) I have not hitherto published any defence, which was directed to the said King, or might directly concern him, which thing notwithstanding I do at this present and declare thereby, that the faults, wherewith the King of Spain mindeth to charge me, belong unto himself.

I do therefore most humbly beseech your Majesty (Sir) that before you judge of this my writing, you would consider the quality both of the crime: and also the quality of mine own person. For, if the King of Spain was content to withhold from me my son and my goods, which he hath in his possession, and further to offer (as at this present he doth) five and twenty thousand crowns for my head, and to promise to make such noble as should murder me, and to pardon them all the faults whatsoever that they could have committed before that time: no man should think it evil in me, that I have attempted by all the means I could, (as indeed heretofore I have done) to preserve my self and mine, and to enable myself what I could, to enter again into that which is mine own: and that I have followed that order and course of life that I have done.[93]

The True Report of the Lamentable Death,
of William of Nassau Prince of Orange:
who was traiterously slain with a Dag in his own Court,
by Balthazar Serack [Gérard] a Burgundian,
the first of July 1584

Herein is expressed the Murderer's confession, and in what manner
he was executed, upon the tenth of the same month. Whose death
was not of sufficient sharpness for such a caitif, and yet too sour
for any Christian . . .

Whoso considereth the state of Princes (although they are as God upon earth, being annointed of God, having their authority from God, and sitting in God's seat to rule the sword with the Law, may perceive that they live in more care and greater danger, than the simplest subject. Lamentable therefore is their late example of the Prince of Orange, slain (by a treacherous villain) in his own Court: his death and the manner thereof, may forewarn other Princes to be careful, whom they retain into the presence of their person. Great is thy loss, and greater will be thy misery (O Flanders,) for the want of thy Prince, who did guide thee and governed thy people, with wisdom, love, policy and continual care for thy quietness: he was thy comfort and the stay of thy state in all extremities.

The chiefest states of thy Country shall miss him: the widow, the sucking babe, and the fatherless child shall have cause to bewail his death. Yea rich and poor, altogether may lament his mishap, and cry woe upon that man that bereaved him of life, whose nobleness deserved fame, and whose worthy acts and enterprises, being honourable, are meet to be registered among the most laudable reports of learned Historiographers. If the Romans did bemoan the death of Caesar, the

Trojans the loss of Hector and the Lacedemonians the want of Alexander, then hast thou (O Flanders) more cause to lament the loss of thy good Prince, who with wisdome, force, and great care, (aided by the power and providence of God himself) did keep thy country, from the hands of him that would make a Monarchy of Realms in his own hands: to the utter spoil of thee and thine, and to draw other Realms under his subjection. O most accursed wretch that he was, so subject to the subtleties of Satan, to work the untimely death of so gracious a Prince, that he thereto hath defended your liberties, and maintained your right these many years, to the great glory of God, the advancement of true Religion. It were too tedious to set down in what subjection all the Low Countries of Flanders, hath been many years yoked in by their enemies: the effect whereof is so notorious and apparent to all the world and the same so truly laid open by many, that it is here needless to touch it: as also to handle the great care of this Prince from time to time, who continually fought to maintain your liberties and to defend your Country from extreme misery: which doubtless hath sharply pinched you: and now having lost him who was the principal prop of the Low Countries, it is like to fall out to the utter overthrow, ruin, and destruction of that poor communality, (a matter most lamentable) except God (the only defender of those that trust in him) do speedily procure and stir up, a careful and godly Prince to be the defender of that people and Country, that thereby the Towns and Villages there about may become populous and thoroughly replenished (now grievously impoverished through civil dissention) to the quietness, wealth, and peace of the same.

And considering it is most necessary to publish a true discourse of this late lamentable mishap, I have thought it good briefly and plainly to set down the true circumstance thereof: and that for one special cause, which is, that considering the untrue imaginations and feigned reports of this Prince's death, now blazed abroad, as well to his friends as to his enemies: the truth being laid open, and made manifest to all men, that then those reports may be accounted frivolous and so be trodden under foot. I therefore admonish you, O ye people of Flanders, that having lost the stay and staff of your country, that you yet vouchsafe with patience to remain content with GOD'S works, who provideth wonderfully for you. It is your sins that is the cause of all your care:

wherefore call upon God in this your time of affliction: and with prayer and hearty repentance, to turn unto the Lord, who no doubt will deliver you from danger: as he did the children of Israel, and assure your selves, that he will so establish your country in short time, pouring thereon peace and plenty, that the remembrance of your great extremity now fallen upon you, shall in short time grow out of memory and be made a flourishing commonwealth which God the father with all speede grant to confirm. Amen.

The discourse of the Treason wrought against William of Nassau, Prince of Orange, by Balthazar Serack, a base born Gentleman of Burgundy, of the age of 25 years

Upon the 12th day of June last past 1584, there came to the Prince of Orange a base born Gentleman of Burgundy, who brought certain Letters from the States of France, concerning matters of news, touching the death of the French king's brother, who died a little before: which Letters, the Prince in most thankful manner did receive, and gave the messenger such friendly entertainment in his own Court, as became a Prince in such cases. The Prince liking well of this messenger, would sundry times use conference with him, touching the garrison of the Prince of Parma, whose soldiers greatly impoverished the countries round about. This messenger (in whom there remained nothing but subtlety and secret mischief) did show unto the Prince, how he could at any time bring him or his soldiers into the Prince of Parma's garrison, where he might take the advantage of the Prince of Parma's power, for that this messenger being a cunning penman, could finely counterfeit the Prince of Parma's own hand, so near that the one should not be known from the other. The Prince notwithstanding would not so deal by his devise, but yet he would enquire of him how all things stood, as well in the Prince of Parma's garrison, as of the Prince's pretence towards the Low Countries, who continually certified unto the Prince of Orange the truth, which caused the Prince to repose a greater trust and confidence in him, so that he remained in the court without suspicion of any treachery. But behold what followed, on the 1st day of July last past, which by the new computation of the Romish Church, was the tenth day of the same month, this Traitor thus harboured and lodged in the Court of this good Prince, seeing a small Pistoll or Dag in the hands of one of the Prince's servants, did demand what it might cost him, saying: I have occasion to ride a journey shortly, and that dag would be a good defence for me upon the highway side, wherefore he requested the Prince's servant that he might buy it of him, who thinking nothing of that which happened afterward, did sell it to him for the sum of 10 shillings of English money. The Prince then being in his Court at Delft, (a town of great strength, where the chiefest States do inhabit), who being gone to dinner, and the Guard attendant about his person, this Traitor seeing it a meet time to compass his pretended mischief (which was, to bereave the Prince of his life, as he did) went into his Chamber, and charged the Pistol with powder, and put three bullets in the same: that done he placed it privily in his pocket, and went down to dinner: who after he had dined, hearing that the Prince would anon go up into his privy chamber, devised in his mind where he might best plant himself, for the finishing of his wicked intent, who finding a privy corner upon the stairs, where he might be shadowed and not be seen, placed himself until the Prince's coming.

The Prince, so soon as he had dined, (which was between one and two of the clock in the afternoon) came forth of the great chamber, with his Lady and Gentlewomen attendant, his Lady purposing to walk abroad, took her leave of the Prince, who going towards the stairs which did lead to the privy chamber, and seeing an Italian named Master Carinson, who had stayed to speak with the Prince, to whom the Prince very friendly spake, saying: Carinson welcome, and took him by the hand, willing this Italian that he should go up with him into his privy chamber, purposing there to use some conference with the Italian Gentleman: and before the Prince entered the stairs, there came an English Captain, called Captain [Roger] Williams, who doing reverence unto the Prince, was entertained in most friendly manner, laying his hand upon Captain Williams' head, willing him also to come up with him.

The Guard then attendant upon the Prince: Master Carinson and Captain Williams followed: But the Prince going up the stairs, not thinking of any such matter as happened, no sooner came directly against this villainous traitor, but he presently discharged his Pistol, wherein (as before mentioned) he having put 3 bullets, two of those bullets went through the Prince's body, and the third remained in his belly, through which wicked stroke, the Prince fell down suddenly, crying out, saying 'Lord have mercy upon me, and remember thy little flock'.

Wherewith he changed this life, to the great grief of his Lady, who greatly lamented his death, as also to the great sorrow of the whole country. The Guard pursued the murderer and sought to slay him, but he overscaped the first Guard, and was stayed by the second watch Guard, which was within the Prince's court.

When he was taken, they demanded of him what he had done, who very obstinately answered, that he had done that thing, which he would willingly do if it were to do again. Then they demanded of him for what cause he did it, he answered, for the cause of his Prince and country: more confession at that time they could not get of him. Forthwith they committed him to prison, where he remained alive to the pleasure of the Estates of the country, who shortly after devised a torment (by death) for this murderer, which was reasonably sharp, yet not so terrible as he deserved.

Grievous was the cry of the people that came flocking to the Prince's gates, to hear the report and truth of what had happened, which known, every household was filled with sorrow, who poured forth their plaints, and did shed tears, for the loss of so good a Christian, as so careful a Prince.

The murderer while he remained in prison, was sundry times examined by the chief Estates of the country, upon whose procurement he committed the said fact, who answered: at the Prince of Parma's request, and other Princes, at whose hands he should receive for doing the same 25,000 Crowns.

The order of the torment, and death of the murderer, was as followeth, which was four days. He had the 1st day the Strappado, openly in the Market. The second day whipped and salted, and his right hand cut off. The third day, his breasts cut out and salt thrown in, and then his left hand cut off. The last day of his torment, which was the 10th of July, he was bound to 2 stakes, standing upright, in such order that he could not stir any way. Thus standing naked, there was a great fire placed some small distance from him, wherein was heated pincers of Iron, with which pincers, two men appointed for the same, did pinch and pull his flesh in smal pieces from his bones, throughout most parts of his body. Then was he unbound from the stakes, and laid upon the earth, and again fastened to four posts, namely by his feet and arms: then they ripped up his belly at which time he had life and perfect memory, he had his bowels burned before his face, and his body cut in four several quarters. During the whole time of his execution, he remained impenitent and obstinate, rejoicing that he had slain the Prince.

Upon the 16th day of July, the Prince was very royally buried, in the new Church at Delft, being lapped in searcloth and Lead, according to the manner of other Princes in time past . . .

God for his mercy send quietness in those parts, that the people may enjoy their own, to the health, wealth, and comfort of them all now distressed. Amen.[94]

Sir Edmund Neville's Testimony Against Dr William Parry
Edmund Neville his declaration the 10 of February 1584.
Subscribed with his own hand.

William Parry the last summer, soon after his repulse in his suit for the Mastership of St Katherine's, repaired to my lodging in the white Friars, where he showed himself a person greatly discontented, and vehemently inveighed against her Majesty, and willed me to assure myself, that during this time and state, I should never receive contentment. But sith, said he, I know you to be honourably descended, and a man of resolution, if you will give me assurance, either to join with me, or not to discover me, I will deliver unto you the only means to do yourself good. Which when I had promised him, he appointed me to come the next day to his house in Fetter Lane: and repairing thither accordingly, I found him in his bed, whereupon he commanded his men forth, and began with me in this order. My lord, said he (for so he called me) I protest before God, that three reasons principally do induce me to enter into this action which I intend to discover unto you: The replanting of religion, The preferring of the Scottish Title, and The advancement of Justice, wonderfully corrupted in this Commonwealth. And thereupon entered into some discourses, what places were fit to be taken to give entrance to such foreign forces as should be best liked of for the furtherance of such enterprises as were to be undertaken.

And with these discourses, he passed the time until he went to dinner: after which, the company being retired, he entered into his former discourses. And if I be not deceived, (said he) by taking of Quinborough Castle, we shall hinder the passage of the queen's ships forth of the River. Whereunto when he saw me use no contradiction, he shook me by the hand, Truth, said he, this is nothing: If we were resolute, there is an enterprise of much more moment, and much easier to perform: An Act honourable, and meritorious to God and the world. Which seeing me desirous to know, he was not ashamed to utter in plain terms, to consist in killing her Majesty: wherein, saith he, if you will go with me, I will lose my life, or deliver my Country from her bad and tyrannous government.

At which speeches finding me discontented, he asked me if I had read Doctor Allen's book, out of which he alleged an authority for it. I answered, No, and that I did not believe that authority. Well said he, what will you say, if I show further authority than this, even from Rome itself, a plain dispensation for the killing of her, wherein you shall find it (as I said before) meritorious. Good cousin, said I, when you shall show it me, I shall think it very strange, when I shall see one to hold that for meritorious, which another holdeth for damnable. Well, saide Parry, do me but the favour to think upon it till tomorrow: and if one man be in the town, I will not fail to show you the thing itself: and if he be not, he will be within these five or six days, at which time if it please you to meet me at Cannon Row, we may there receive the Sacrament to be true each to the other and then I will discover unto you both the party, and then the thing itself. Whereupon I prayed Parry to think better upon it, as a matter of great charge both of soul and body. I would to God, said Parry, you were as perfectly persuaded in it as I am, for then undoubtedly you should do God great service.

Not long after 8 or 9 days, (as I remember) Parry coming to visit me at my lodging in Hern's rents in Holborn, as he often used, we walked forth into the fields, where he renewed again his determination to kill her Majesty, whom he said he thought most unworthy to live, and that he wondered I was so scrupulous therein. She hath sought, said he, your ruin and overthrow, why should you not then seek to revenge it? I confess, quoth I, that my case is hard, but yet I am not so desperate as to revenge it upon myself, which must needs be the event of so unhonest and unpossible an enterprise. Unpossible, said Parry, I wonder at you, for in truth there is not anything more easy: you are no Courtier and therefore know not her customs of walking with small train, and often in the garden very privately, at which time myself may easily have access unto her, and you also when you are known in Court. Upon the fact we must have a barge ready to carry us with speed down the river, where we will have a ship ready to transport us if it be needful: but upon my head, we shall never be followed so far.

I asked him, How will you escape forth of the garden? For you shall not be permitted to carry any men with you, and the gates will then be locked, neither can you carry a Dag without suspicion. As for a Dag, said Parry, I care not: my Dagger is enough. And as for my escaping, those that shall be with her, will be so busy about her, as I shall find opportunity enough to escape, if you be there ready with the barge to receive me. But if this seems dangerous in respect of your reason before showed, let it then rest till her coming to St James, and let us furnish our selves in the mean time with men and horse fit for the purpose: we may each of us keep eight or ten men without suspicion. And for my part, said he, I shall find good fellows that will follow me without suspecting mine intent.

It is much, said he, that so many resolute men may do upon the sudden, being well appointed with each his Case of Dags: if they were an hundred waiting upon her, they were not able to save her, you coming of the one side, and I on the other, and discharging our Dags upon her, it were unhappy if we should both miss her. But if our Dags fail, I shall bestir me well with a sword ere she escape me. Whereunto I said, Good Doctor, give over this odious enterprise, and trouble me no more with the hearing of that, which in heart I loathe so much. I would to God the enterprise were honest, that I might make known unto thee whether I want resolution. And not long after, her Majesty came to Saint James, after which, one morning (the day certain I remember not,) Parry revived again his former discourse of killing her Majesty, with greater earnestness and importunity persuading me to join therein: saying he thought me the only man in England like to performe it, in respect of my valour, as he termed it.[95]

A Proclamation against the common use of Dags, Handguns, Arquebuses, Callibers, and Cotes of Defence

The Queen's Majesty, being informed credibly from sundry parts of the Realm, that her former commandments, contained in her Proclamations heretofore published for the prohibiting of the common carrying of Dags, Pistols, and such other short pieces of shot according to the Acts of Parliament remaining of force, have not been by such public Officers in Shires, Towns, and other public places duly executed, as by the said proclamations was ordered, but have in a generality been neglected, and so the disorder grown so great in common carrying of Dags, Pistols, and such like, not only in Cities and Towns, and in all parts of the Realm in common highways, whereby her Majesty's good quiet people, desirous to live in peaceable manner, are in fear and danger of their lives to travel abroad for their necessary business, by means of the multitude of the evil disposed, who contrary to the Laws and her Majesty's proclamations do so commonly carry such offensive weapons, being in time of peace only meet for thieves, robbers and murderers: Whereupon her Majesty by the advice of the Council, and upon the general complaint made of the mutitude of her peaceable people, doth give straight charge to all manner officers, to whom the execution of the former proclamations did appertain, that immediately upon the publication hereof, they do with speed take order how the contents of the foresaid proclamations may be speedily put in due execution. And to that end her Majesty chargeth all Mayors, Sheriffs, Bailiffs, and other head Officers of Cities and towns corporate, and all Justices of Peace within all Counties and other places having any special liberties, that they do assemble themselves in some accustomed places, and there to set down certain order, and appoint special ministers, not only to enquire of the default of the execution of the foresaid Proclamations, but also to proceed duly to the execution thereof.

And furthermore, where her Majesty understandeth that besides the

enormities grown by lack of execution of the said Proclamations against
the common usage of Dags and Pistols, there is another greater disorder
grown of common carrying abroad both in Towns and fields, of great
Pieces, as Arquebuses, Callibers and such like, under colour of learning
or exercising to shoot therein, to the service at Musters appointed in
sundry Counties for the common service of the Realm, (a matter to be
in good sort favoured, but not to be misused) by which means, through
the general carrying of them in places not appointed for such musters,
and by the frequent shooting with them in and near Cities, Towns
corporate, or the Suburbs thereof where great multitude of people do
live, reside, and travel up and down for their necessary business, many
harms do ensue, and occasions like encrease of great danger, by such
liberty permitted for the use of such offensive weapons in places not
convenient. For these considerations, and for the consequences of sundry mischiefs that may ensue, her Majesty by like advice of her Council,
doth command and charge all manner her subjects of what estate so
ever they be, from henceforth to forbear from shooting in any manner
of Handguns, Arquebuses, Callibers, or such like, of what name so ever
they be, either charged with Bullet or without, in any place, but only
at and in the places that are or shall be appointed for common Musters,
by the direction of the Commissioners for general Musters, or else at
and in such places as are, or shall be appointed to be meet places,
either within great Cities or the Suburbs of the same, or in places far
off from Towns of habitation, for the exercise of Shooting in such
pieces as is aforesaid, and for the learning to shoot in the same places.
And that no such Piece be charged with Shot or Powder, but at, or in
the same place so limited for Musters, or for exercise of Shooting. And
if persons being Artificers, makers of such Pieces in any place, shall
have cause to try such Pieces, either for the satisfaction of themselves,
or of any that shall desire to buy the same, the trial thereof shall also
be at the said places so limited, and at none other. And if any person
shall hereafter attempt the contrary, to the breach of these her Highness's commandments, that the same shall be committed to prison, by
any Officer having charge to see the keeping of the Peace, or being any
principal or chief Officers of Ordinance or Castles where any Ordinance
is kept, that shall be next to the same place, there to remain. And upon
any second Offence to be committed to close Prison, and there to

remain until the same shall be expressely bailed by commandment of her Majesty, or of six of her Privy Council.

Furthermore, her Majesty in like sort commandeth, that no manner of Person shall use any Shooting in any such small Pieces, within two miles of any house where her Majesty shall reside, during the times of her Majesty's residing, upon like pain as before is expressed. And to that end her Majesty chargeth her Marshall of her house, to be careful by himself and his Ministers, to see the due observation thereof. And if he shall find any to offend therein, not only to commit the same to prison, but also to advertise her Majesty, or her Privy Council thereof, that some further extraordinary punishment may be extended upon such audacious persons as shall adventure to offend so near to the place, where her Majesty's person shall be.

And whereas divers of late years have used to wear privy Coats, and Doublets of defence, thereby intending to quarrel, and make affrays upon other unarmed, and presume audaciously to apparel themselves with the said privy Armour, not only in Cities, Towns, and public assembly, but within her Majesty's Court wheresoever, to the great offence and contempt of her Highness, and of her Laws, and to the hurt of divers her Majesty's good subjects. Therefore her Majesty doth expressly prohibit and forbid all and every of her subjects whatsoever, the wearing of any such Privy or secret kind of Coat, or Doublet of Defence. And further her Majesty's express pleasure is, that all her Justices of peace, Mayors, Sheriffs, Bailiffs, Constables, and other her Majesty's Officers whatsoever, shall and may lawfully apprehend and arrest all such persons, as shall offend contrary to the Tenor of this Proclamation in that behalf. And the said persons so apprehended, shall, and may lawfully commit to the next prison and gaol, where they shall be so arrested, there to remain without bail or mainprise, until there shall be direction given from her Majesty's Privy Council. And the same privy Coats or Doublets to be taken from them, and sent to the Sheriff of the shire for the time being, to be by him kept until her Majesty shall otherwise dispose of the same. And the party so offending to be fined at her Highness's will and pleasure.

Finally, also her Majesty farther chargeth all manner Officers in Cities, Towns and other places, to make search for all manner small Dags, called pocket Dags, as well in any man's house to be suspected for the same, as in the Shops and Houses of Artificers that do use to make the same: And all them shall seize and take into their custody, delivering a Bill of their hands, testifying the receipt thereof, to the intent the owners may have such recompense for the same, as hereafter upon Certificate to her Majesty's Privy Council, or to the Presidents and Councils in Wales and in the North parts, shall be thought requisite. And herewith her Majesty commandeth, that no manner of person shall hereafter either make or amend, or shall bring into this Realm, any such Dags, commonly called pocket Dags, or such like, upon pain of imprisonment, as next above is expressed. And wheresoever there are any persons that have made any small Shot, the same shall be bound in reasonable sums to her Majesty's use, by the discretion of the principal Officers of the Town, not to make nor put to Sale, or otherwise to utter any such small Pieces as are commonly called pocket Dags, or that may be hid in any Pocket, or like place about a man's body, to be hid or carried covertly.

And for execution of all the contents of this Proclamation, her Majesty chargeth all her Officers, that either in Liberties or without, have any authority to enquire of the breach of her Majesty's peace, to assemble themselves presently, and so monthly between this and Christmas next. And there by a Jury of sufficient persons to be sworn, or by other ministers to be by them deputed, to enquire of the observation of all the points herein contained.[96]

NOTES

1 '*La politique dans une oeuvre
littéraire c'est un coup de pistolet
au milieu d'un concert, quelque
chose de grossier et auquel
pourtant il n'est pas possible de
refuser son attention. Nous allons
parler de fort vilaines choses.*'

2 First verse of the 'Wilhelmus',
the Dutch national anthem. The
first and sixth verses of this
fifteen-verse poem are usually
sung, linking William of
Orange's name with Spain and
opposition to tyranny:
'*Wilhelmus van Nassouwe/ben ik
van Duitsen bloed/den vaderland
getrouwe/blijf ik tot in den dood./
Een Prinse van Oranje/ben ik, vrij
onverveerd,/den Koning van
Hispanje/heb ik altijd geëerd.//
Mijn schild ende betrouwen/zijt
Gij, o God mijn Heer,/op U zo wil
ik bouwen,/verlaat mij
nimmermeer./Dat ik doch vroom
mag blijven,/uw dienaar t'aller
stond,/de tirannie verdrijven/die
mij mijn hert doorwondt.*' The
poem was composed in 1568,
supposedly by William the
Silent's friend and counsellor
Marnix van St-Aldegonde. The
phrase '*van Duitsen bloed*' in the
first verse, which originally

referred to William's German
parentage, is nowadays
conveniently rendered 'Dutch' in
translations. 'In the
"Wilhelmus", the composer
depicts the Prince addressing the
oppressed people of the
Netherlands . . . and expounds
his innermost motives for rising
against the King of Spain. Prince
William comforts his followers,
but at the same time exhorts
them to join in the struggle. He
also reminds them of their duty
to obey God . . . The tune of the
"Wilhelmus" is based on a
French soldier's song, which was
popular around 1568 and
alternates between three/four and
four/four time . . . The melody
was further developed by
Adriaen Valerius (*c*.1575–1625).
The oldest copy of the
"Wilhelmus" is to be found in
Deuchdelijke Solutien (Antwerp,
1574). Since 1626, it has been
included in Valerius's
Gedenckclanck, a well known
collection of national songs.'
(Wilhelmus website). In Dutch
the first letters of the
Wilhelmus's fifteen stanzas spell
out 'Willem van Nassav'.

3 The Orangemen, in those familiar House of Orange colours, who parade annually from 12 July, do so to commemorate William III's victory over James II at the Battle of the Boyne in 1690, which was the final step in clinching William's claim to the English throne.

4 Princeton, which was first settled in the seventeenth century, was named in honour of William III of Orange, also William of Nassau. The main street in the town is Nassau Street. The central hall of the university which was established there half a century later in 1745 (as the College of New Jersey) was originally Nassau Hall.

5 Jack Ruby shot and killed John F. Kennedy's alleged assassin, Lee Harvey Oswald, with a handgun as he was brought from jail to the courtroom, thereby removing forever the possibility of finding out whether Oswald was indeed the killer, and if so, whether he was working alone. In a fresh move in 2004, the FBI announced that digital analysis and cleaning up of a piece of audio from a police outrider close to Kennedy's car might even now allow investigators to decide how many shots were actually fired, and whether from one gun or two. Thus guns and gunshots continue to dominate the story of Kennedy's assassination.

6 This account of William's early

life and career draws on Alistair Duke's introductory essay, 'From "Loyal Servant" to "Irreconcilable Opponent" of Spain: Koenraad Swart's Interpretation of William of Orange, 1533–72', in K.W. Swart, *William of Orange and the Revolt of the Netherlands, 1572–84*, trans. J.C. Grayson (Aldershot: Ashgate, 2003), pp.8–24, and on H.H. Rowen, *The Princes of Orange: The Stadholders in the Dutch Republic* (Cambridge: Cambridge University Press, 1988).

7 Charles arranged the advantageous marriage for the seventeen-year-old William to Anne of Egmont, heiress of the Count of Buren. Anne died in 1558, having given birth to a son and heir, Philip William, Prince of Orange and Count of Buren, and a daughter, Maria.

8 As it turned out, this marriage, which produced three children, including Maurice, the next Dutch stadholder Prince of Orange, was a deeply unhappy one. Anna fled from Dillenberg Castle shortly after Maurice's birth. 'Two years later she was arrested in Cologne for living in adultery with Jan Rubens (who later became the father of the painter Peter Paul Rubens), imprisoned, and her marriage to William formally dissolved in 1574. She died in 1577 at her ancestral home in Dresden.' (Rowen, *Princes of Orange*, p.37.)

9 Swart, 'Willem van Oranje en de

Nederlandse Opstand', p.106, cit. Swart, *William of Orange*, p.21.

10 This account of the complex international events impinging on the outcome of Orange's 1572 incursion is based on Israel, *The Dutch Republic*; Geyl, *History of the Dutch Speaking Peoples*; Parker, *The Dutch Revolt*.

11 Parker, *The Dutch Revolt*, p.137.

12 Cit. ibid., pp.137–8.

13 'Bartholomew's Day massacre', Catholic Encyclopedia online, http://www.newadvent.org/ cathen/13333b.htm.

14 Swart, *William of Orange*, p.23.

15 Ibid., pp.30–1, 144–7.

16 For the full text see Kossman and Mellink, *Texts Concerning the Revolt of the Netherlands*, pp.98–100.

17 Israel, *The Dutch Republic*, p.178.

18 Requescens to Zuñiga, 12 November 1575, cit. Parker, *The Army of Flanders and the Spanish Road*, p.235.

19 See Parker, *The Army of Flanders and the Spanish Road*; Darby, *The Origins and Development of the Dutch Revolt*, p.120.

20 Swart, *William of Orange*, p.220. For the complete set of images of the 'joyous entry', widely circulated throughout Europe at the time, see *La ioyeuse et magnifique entrée de Monseigneur Françoys fils de France . . . en sa tres-renommée ville d'Anvers* (Antwerp, 1582). Herle sent a copy to Walsingham.

21 Cit. Swart, *William of Orange*, p.234.

22 See Rowen, *Princes of Orange*, p.27.

23 In the period of this book Continental Europe used the revised calendar, while England continued to use the old one. Thus dates in the Low Countries run ten calendar days ahead of those in England. Where the events I describe centre on the Low Countries (as here) I give the Continental version of the date. Where they focus on England I give dates in their English form. Where both England and the Low Countries are involved I specify the date form used.

24 For the terms of Philip II's announcement of the price on William the Silent's head see Appendix 1.

25 Calendar of State Papers, Foreign Series, Elizabeth, July 1583–July 1584, ed. Sophie Crawford Lomas, Endd. Fr. 1 pp. [Holl. and Fl. XXII, 28].

26 Vuillafans is undecided as to whether its infamous son is a hero or a villain. When I visited in 2004 a local resident helpfully told me Gérard's story, and then enquired delicately whether I was a Catholic (in which case he was clearly ready to hail him as a hero). Finding I was not, he was rather more cautious in explaining that Gérard had carried out William's assassination because of his family's passionate commitment to Philip II.

27 On Villiers see C. Boer, *Hofpredikers an Prins Willem van Oranje. Jean Taffin en Pierre*

Loyseleur de Villiers (The Hague: M. Nijhoff, 1952).

28 Endd. Fr. 1 pp. [Holl. and Fl. XXII. 28.] p.587 1584 July 4/14. 721. Torture and Execution of Balthazar Gérard.

29 PRO SP 83 15/88. William Herle to the Earl of Leicester, 31 March 1582. I am very grateful to Dr Robyn Adams for allowing me to use her transcriptions of these and other Herle-related documents.

30 Calendar of State Papers, Relating to English Affairs, Preserved Principally in the Archives of Samancas, Vol. III, 1580–1586, 1582 1 April. 238. Mendoza to Philip II, pp.324–8.

31 There is an extremely partisan account of the 1582 attempt on William's life, by A. de Meyer O.P., whose sole purpose is to exonerate Antonin Temmerman from blame. Meyer argues that Jauregay would never have told the priest of the planned assassination, and that, besides, it is not permissible for a priest to give absolution for a crime not yet committed. Although the book is absurdly partisan, it contains full original archival materials from the Antwerp and Plantin records. See A. de Meyer, *Le procès de l'attentat commis contre Guillaume le Taciturne Prince d'Orange 18 mars 1582: Étude critique de documents inédits* (Brussels: L'Édition Universelle, 1933).

32 Herle seems later to have been reprimanded for exaggerating the gravity of William's condition at this early stage. He retaliated by continuing to maintain that the Prince really had almost died, despite bulletins being issued to the contrary. Both in 1582 and 1584, however, Herle's dispatches urged the Queen to send troops, immediately following the attempted assassination; his spy-masters were more circumspectly for limited English involvement in the Netherlands, hence the reprimand.

33 PRO SP 83/15/128. William Herle to Sir Francis Walsingham, 28 April 1582.

34 Calendar of State Papers, Domestic, Elizabeth, 1581–1590, ed. Robert Lemon, p.55. 1582 May 19. (Vol. CLIII) p. 54. Herle to Walsingham.

35 B.S. Hall, *Weapons and Warfare in Renaissance Europe* (Baltimore: The Johns Hopkins University Press, 1997), p.191. This technical account of the wheel-lock pistol and its impact on sixteenth-century warfare is taken directly from Hall.

36 'In western Europe the demise of heavy cavalry was not mainly a result of the spread of arquebuses, or even muskets, among infantry troops. Rather, it took place fairly suddenly in the second half of the sixteenth century as a direct consequence of the spread of the wheel-lock pistol.' Ibid., p.190.

37 Ibid., pp.190–1.

38 Ibid., p.194.

39 See pp. 130–1.

40 Cit. Hall, *Weapons and Warfare*, pp.195–6.

41 Conyers Read, *Mr Secretary Walsingham and the Policy of Queen Elizabeth* (Oxford: Clarendon Press, 1925), II, p.358.

42 'Another Frenchman who rendered the Prince great services at this time was the prominent Huguenot François de la Noue, an extremely talented commander, who for a time relieved Orange of much of the burden of his task as commander in chief of the State's army. In him the Prince at last found a man who was not the inferior of the Spanish generals, and his capture in May 1580 was not the least of the many reverses that Orange had to endure in his years at Antwerp' (Swart, *William of Orange*, p.146).

43 On Norris see J.S. Nolan, *Sir John Norreys and the Elizabethan Military World* (Exeter: University of Exeter Press, 1997).

44 Hall, *Weapons and Warfare*, p.215.

45 De la Noue wrote his *Discours politiques et militaires* during his imprisonment. It was published in French and English in 1587.

46 H.L. Blackmore, *A Dictionary of London Gunmakers 1350–1850* (Oxford: Phaidon & Christie's, 1986).

47 On Essex, see cover of P.E.J. Hammer, *The Polarisation of Elizabethan Politics: The Political Career of Robert Devereux, 2nd Earl of Essex, 1585–1597* (Cambridge: Cambridge University Press, 1999).

48 Painted 1594. My thanks to Karen Hearn for the reference and description of the painting. 'Thomas was related to Sir Henry Lee, Elizabeth I's Champion and creator of imagery for her annual Accession Day celebrations. Henry may have helped devise the complex symbolism of this portrait. Thomas served in the English colonial forces in Ireland. His bare legs are a fantasy evocation both of the dress of an Irish soldier, and that of a Roman hero. Thomas was suspected of treachery to Elizabeth and visited London in 1594 partly to refute this. The Latin inscription in the tree refers to the Roman Mucius Scaevola, who stayed true to Rome even when among its enemies. Lee implies that he too is faithful' (caption taken from Tate Britain website).

49 S. Adams (ed.), *Household Accounts and Disbursement Books of Robert Dudley, Earl of Leicester: 1558–1561, 1584–1586*, Camden Fifth Series, vol. 6 (Cambridge: Cambridge University Press, 1995), p.260.

50 January 1560 [1561]. 'Lewes' was Lewis Byllyard, who later worked for the queen (Blackmore, *A Dictionary of London Gunmakers*, p.2).

51 Nolan, *Sir John Norreys*, p.89.

52 Ibid., pp.99–101.

53 'French Fury' engraving reproduced in ibid., p.58.

54 Montaigne believed he had been shot in the head with an

arquebus. See reference in L.F. Parmelee, *Good Newes from Fraunce: French Anti-League Propaganda in Late Elizabethan England* (Rochester, NY: University of Rochester Press, 1996), p.59.

55 John Webster, *The White Devil*, Act V, Scene vi.

56 I am grateful to Rachel Jardine for allowing me to use her MA essay on the Belchamp Hall pistol, submitted in 1999 for the MA course in Early History of Design at the RCA and V&A.

57 James Aske, *Elizabetha Triumphans* (London, 1588), p.8.

58 BL MS Lansdowne 39 f.193^{r-v}. William Herle to Lord Burghley, 16 November 1583.

59 Calendar of the Manuscripts of the Most Hon. The Marquis of Salisbury . . . preserved at Hatfield House, Pt. III, ed. S.R. Scargill-Bird, p.44, 1584, July 17. 93, p.45. Sent from Paris – original in French S.P., vol. lxxx.

60 See R.J. Adams, ' "Both Diligent and Secret": The Intelligence Letters of William Herle' (unpublished PhD dissertation, University of London, 2004).

61 For the various plots against Elizabeth see John Guy, *Tudor England* (Oxford: Oxford University Press, 1988); Read, *Mr Secretary Walsingham*, II.

62 Read, *Mr Secretary Walsingham*, II, p.381.

63 Ibid.

64 Secret advertisement from Exeter, not dated. S.P. Domestic, clxxxv, no. 53, cit. ibid.

65 Lansdowne MSS. 39, f. 21, cit. ibid., p.400.

66 John Bossy thinks it likely that Parry really did intend to assassinate Elizabeth. See Bossy, *Under the Molehill*, p.96.

67 *A Trve and plaine declaration of the horrible Treasons, practised by William Parry the Traitor, against the Queenes Maiestie. The maner of his Arraignment, Conuiction and execution, together with the copies of sundry letters of his and others, tending to diuers purposes, for the proofes of his Treason* (London, 1585), p.5.

68 'To the Q most | Excellent Mati:/| 22. Iulij 1584 | Wm Herle fro Amsterda'. Transcriptions of William Herle's letters by Robyn Adams.

69 p.606 1584 July 12. 746. Fr. 1 pp. [SPF Entry Book 162, p.118.]

70 Cit. Nolan, *Sir John Norreys*, p.13.

71 *Leicester Correspondence*, p.viii.

72 Israel, *The Dutch Republic*, p.219.

73 For the early approach to Anjou see M. van Gelderen, *The Political Thought of the Dutch Revolt 1555–1590* (Cambridge: Cambridge University Press, 1992), p.53; M.P. Holt, *The Duke of Anjou and the Politique Struggle During the Wars of Religion* (Cambridge: Cambridge University Press, 1986). For William's proposal to Elizabeth see William Herle's Discourse on Flanders (transcribed by Robyn Adams).

74 SP 70 127/36 (173^r – 181^v [a booklet, blank after 181^r until 184^v]) William Herle's Discourse

on Flanders. See also BL MS Cotton Titus F III f. 295ʳ – 301ᵛ – copy, annotated briefly by Herle. See also BL MS Cotton Galba C IV, f.381–8. My thanks to Robyn Adams for giving me access to her transcription of this document.

75 *Leicester Correspondence*, p.76.
76 Read, *Mr Secretary Walsingham*, I, pp.324–5.
77 R.C. Strong and J.A. van Dorsten, *Leicester's Triumph* (Leiden and London: Leiden and Oxford University Press, 1964), pp.13–14.
78 See Swart, *William of Orange*, pp.129–31; Strong and van Dorsten, *Leicester's Triumph*, pp.7–10 (though they suggest the proposed marriage was to William's sister). On Sidney's prominent role in European Protestantism see A. Stewart, *Philip Sidney: A Double Life* (London: Chatto & Windus, 2000).
79 Swart, *William of Orange*, pp.139–42.
80 See p. 35.
81 Swart, *William of Orange*, p.217.
82 *William Herle's Discourse on Flanders*.
83 Strong and van Dorsten, *Leicester's Triumph*, p.33.
84 See Hammer, *The Polarisation of Elizabethan Politics*, pp.39ff.
85 Cit. Strong and van Dorsten, *Leicester's Triumph*, p.35.
86 *Leicester Correspondence*, pp.58–9.

87 Nolan, *Sir John Norreys*, p.99.
88 Hammer, *The Polarisation of Elizabethan Politics*, p.70.
89 Ibid., p.76.
90 Harvey's copy of Frontinus also includes a direct reference to 'My L. of Leicester now in the Low Countries'.
91 Lyrics as recorded by Bob Dylan, Columbia Studios, New York, NY, 7 August 1963; performed at Greenwood, Mississippi, 6 July 1963; March on Washington, 28 August 1963. © 1963, 1964 Warner Bros. Inc. © Renewed 1991 Special Rider Music.
92 H. Wansink, *The Apologie of Prince William of Orange against the Proclamation of the King of Spaine* (Leiden: E.J. Brill, 1969), pp.150–69.
93 Ibid., pp.1–3.
94 Sig. A.2ᵛ. BL C.40.a.34.
95 *A Trve and plaine declaration . . .*, pp.7–10.
96 'Given at our Manor of Greenwich, the 26th day of July in the 21st year of our reign. God saue the Queen. Imprinted in London at Bacon House by Christopher Barker, Printer to the Queen's Majesty. Anno 1579'. *A Booke Containing All Svch Proclamations, As Were Pvblished Dvring the Raigne of the late Queene Elizabeth. Collected Together by the industry of Humfrey Dyson, of the City of London Publique Notary . . .* (London, 1618), f.189.

FURTHER READING

R.J. Adams, ' "Both Diligent and Secret": The Intelligence Letters of William Herle' (unpublished PhD dissertation, University of London, 2004)

S.L. Adams, 'The Protestant Cause: Religious Alliance with the West European Calvinist Communities as a Political Issue in England 1585–1603' (unpublished DPhil thesis, University of Oxford, 1973)

H.L. Blackmore, *A Dictionary of London Gunmakers 1350–1850* (Oxford: Phaidon & Christie's, 1986)

J. Bossy, *Under the Molehill: An Elizabethan Spy Story* (New Haven and London: Yale University Press, 2001)

J. Bruce (ed.) *Correspondence of Robert Dudley, Earl of Leycester, during his Government of the Low Countries, in the years 1585 and 1586* (London: AMS Press, 1968)

G. Darby (ed.), *The Origins and Development of the Dutch Revolt* (London: Routledge, 2001)

A.T. van Deursen and H. de Schepper, *Willem van Oranje: een strijd voor vrijheid enverdraagzaamheid* (Weesp, 1984)

I. Eaves, 'Some Notes on the Pistol in Early-17th Century England', JAAS 6 (1968–1970), pp.277–344

I. Eaves, 'Further Notes on the Pistol in Early 17th-Century England', JAAS 8 (1973–1975), pp.269–329

L.-P. Gachard, *Correspondance de Guillaume le Taciturne, prince d'Orange*, 6 vols (Brussels: A. Vandale, 1847–57)

M. van Gelderen, *The Political Thought of the Dutch Revolt 1555–1590* (Cambridge: Cambridge University Press, 1992)

P. Geyl, *The Revolt of the Netherlands 1555–1609* (London, 1932; repr. 1988)

P. Geyl, *History of the Dutch-Speaking Peoples 1555–1648* (London: Phoenix Press, 2001) (which combines the first two volumes of Geyl's incomplete Dutch history: *The Revolt of the Netherlands 1555–1609* and *The Netherlands Divided 1609–1648* (London: Williams and Norgate, 1932, 1936))

J. Guy, *Tudor England* (Oxford: Oxford University Press, 1988)

J.R. Hale, *War and Society in Renaissance Europe 1450–1620* (Stroud: Sutton Publishing, 1985)

B.S. Hall, *Weapons and Warfare in Renaissance Europe* (Baltimore: The Johns Hopkins University Press, 1997)

P.E.J. Hammer, *The Polarisation of Elizabethan Politics: The Political Career of Robert Devereux, 2nd Earl of Essex, 1585–1597* (Cambridge: Cambridge University Press, 1999)

J.F. Hayward, 'English Firearms of the 16th Century', JAAS 3 (1959–1961), pp.117–43

J.F. Hayward, *A Dictionary of London Gunmakers 1350–1850* (London: Phaidon, 1986)

M.P. Holt, *The Duke of Anjou and the Politique Struggle During the Wars of Religion* (Cambridge: Cambridge University Press, 1986)

J.I. Israel, *The Dutch Republic: Its Rise, Greatness, and Fall 1477–1806* (Oxford: Clarendon Press, 1995)

R. Jardine, 'The Belchamp Pistol' (unpublished V&A MA essay)

E.H. Kossmann and A.F. Mellink (eds), *Texts Concerning the Revolt of the Netherlands* (Cambridge: Cambridge University Press, 1967)

J.J. Murray, *Flanders and England: The Influence of the Low Countries on Tudor-Stuart England* (Antwerp: Fonds Mercator, 1985)

J.S. Nolan, *Sir John Norreys and the Elizabethan Military World* (Exeter: University of Exeter Press, 1997)

G. Parker, *The Army of Flanders and the Spanish Road 1567–1659* (Cambridge: Cambridge University Press, 1972)

G. Parker, *The Dutch Revolt* (rev. edn, Harmondsworth: Penguin, 1985)

H.H. Rowen, *The Princes of Orange: The Stadholders in the Dutch Republic* (Cambridge: Cambridge University Press, 1988)

R.C. Strong and J.A. van Dorsten, *Leicester's Triumph* (Leiden and London: Leiden and Oxford University Press, 1964)

N.M. Sutherland, *The Massacre of St Bartholomew and the European Conflict, 1559–1572* (Macmillan: London, 1973)

K.W. Swart, *William of Orange and the Revolt of the Netherlands, 1572–84*, trans. J.C. Grayson (Aldershot: Ashgate, 2003)

H. Wansink, *The Apologie of Prince William of Orange against the Proclamation of the King of Spaine* (Leiden: E.J. Brill, 1969)

INDEX

'W' indicates Prince William the Silent. Figures in italic refer to illustrations

Act of Abjuration (1581) 43, 48
Aerschot, Duke of 125
Allen, Dr 112, 153
Alva (Alba), Duke of 36, 45, 91, 145:
puts down first Dutch uprising 32;
confiscation of W's Dutch
properties and revenues 32–3; seizes
W's eldest son 33; drives back W's
forces 33; blockade of Mons 34–5,
37, 39; sacking of Mechelen and
Zutphen 39; slaughter at Naarden
39–40; imposition of Spanish rule
and Catholic faith on the Dutch 40;
recalled from the Low Countries
40; Dutch taxation 41
Anastro, Gaspar 68–71
Anglo–Dutch trade: and fall of
Antwerp 121; Herle's offer 122
Anjou, Duke of: secret negotiations
with W 121, 123, 125; becomes titular
ruler of the Low Countries 42–3, 64;
installed at Antwerp as Duke of
Brabant 43–4, *43*, 126; insistence on
public Catholic worship 44; W's
continued defence of 44; and
assassination attempt on W (1582)
64–5, 66, 68, 72; evaporation of
support for 76; distaste for
agreement with France 76; fiasco of
second Antwerp entry ('French
Fury', 1583) 45, *93*, 125, 126; reports
rumours of plot against Elizabeth
100; Elizabeth backs 104, 125; death
46, 48, 52, 56
Anna of Saxony (W's second wife)
29–30, 160n

Antwerp: Charles V's court 26, *27*;
W's household 37; 'Spanish Fury'
41; W moves his headquarters to
42; Anjou installed as Duke of
Brabant (1582) 43–4, *43*; Anjou's
second entry ('French Fury') 45, *93*,
125, 126, 163n; and assassination
attempt on W (1582) 64–6, 71; falls
to the Spanish (1585) 72, 90, 121;
and rumours about Catholic
factions in England 100; ceases
to be hub of Anglo–Dutch trade
121
Arafat, Yassar 48
arquebuses 80, 81, 106, 156
artillery 84
Augustus, Elector of Saxony 30

Babington Plot (1586) 132
Baghdad 113
belt-hook 57, 88, 97
Bilbao 69
Biron, General 46
Boyne, Battle of the (1690) 160n
Brabant, Duchy of 36, 37, 39, 42, 45
Breda 26
Brill 122
Brussels 28
Burghley, William Cecil, 1st Baron 91,
101, 108, 121, 129, 130
Butler, Sir Philip 131
Byllyard, Lewis 163n

calendar 161n
Calvinists 31, 32, 34
caracole manoeuvre 81

Carinson (Italian officer) 50, 149
Catherine de Medici 17–18, 35
Catholic factions 17, 100
Catholicism: of Duke of Anjou 44; demonised as superstitious 68; Parry converts 107; and symbolism of the handgun 112–13
Catholics: antagonism towards Protestants 18; anti-Catholicism in northern Netherlands 30; W's attitude towards 31; anti-Catholic iconoclasm 32; and the Parry plot 107–8
cavalry 80–1, 162n
Chalon estates 26
Charles I, King of England 134
Charles II, King of England 134
Charles V, Holy Roman Emperor: and Chalon estates 26; W spends time in his household 26, 27; resigns the sovereignty of the Netherlands 28; trusts W 28; holds Philip of Hesse prisoner 30; fortification of Mons 34; collection of handguns 96–7, 97
Charles IX, King of France 34, 35
Charlotte of Bourbon (W's third wife) 124
Cockson, Thomas 85
Coligny, Admiral Gaspard de 35–6, 45
Coligny, Louise de (W's fourth wife) 45, 118–20, 134
Counter-Reformation 128

dags see under pistols
de la Noue, François 82–3, 125, 163n
Delft 45, 46, 50, 56, 59, 136, 149, 151
Derby, Edward Stanley, Earl of 91
Deventer 92
Diana, Princess of Wales 132
Dillenburg 26, 160n
Dôle, Catholic University of 55
Dordrecht: political assembly (1572) 37–8; Marnix's speech 38–9
double agents 19
Drake, Sir Francis 132, 133

Duplessis-Mornay, Philippe 37, 45, 47
Dutch national anthem (the 'Wilhelmus') 15, 16, 26, 159n
Dutch Revolt: start of (mid-1560s) 32; W's skill as a negotiator 27; 'League of the Great' engineers Granvelle's removal 33; Elizabeth I's indirect financing of 34, 123; Mons blockade 34–5, 37, 39; sacking of Mechelen and Zutphen 39; slaughter at Naarden 39–40; Philip II's ability to crush 40; 'Spanish Fury' at Antwerp (1575) 41; Parma becomes Governor-General (1578) 42; W wins pamphlet war 47; Philip II outlaws W (1580) 47, 60–1, 120, 144–5; Act of Abjuration (1581) 43, 48; 'French Fury' (Antwerp, 1583) 45, 93, 125, 126, 163n; Antwerp falls to the Spanish 72, 90, 121; assassination of W see under William the Silent; Stanley fights on both sides 92; Elizabeth persuaded to involve herself in 118; Leicester appointed Governor (1586) 129; Spanish Armada defeated (1588) 133–4
Dylan, Bob 135, 165n

Egmont, Count of 33
Elizabeth I, Queen of England 81, 85, 88, 103: refusal to become officially embroiled in Dutch Revolt 122–4; W's part in her policies 16; secret negotiations with W 121; supports W's Dutch Revolt 34, 47, 123; and attempt on W's life 66–7; Accession Day celebrations 163n; and W's death 52, 119–20; appoints Leicester to assist Dutch Protestant cause 88; feared to be in danger 99–102; determined to avoid confrontation with Philip II 104; backs Anjou 104, 125–6; alleged plots against 20, 82–3, 105–12, 132; security forces

Elizabeth I – *contd.*
tighten strangehold after W's murder 114–15; becomes involved in Dutch Revolt 118, 120; and Louise de Coligny 118, 119–20; 'Declaration' (1585) 120–1; professes devotion to Anjou 125–6; and Leicester's acceptance of implied sovereignty in the Netherlands 130
England: political mistrust in 18; forces committed against Spanish Habsburg troops (1585) 16; and launch of Spanish Armada (1588) 16
English aftermath of W's murder: copycat conspiracies and hidden handguns 99–111; psychological warfare 111–15; reeling from the consequences 117–21; furthering English interests 121–6; 'The end of all our ambitions' 127–34
English navy 133, 134
Enkhuisen 122
Essex, Robert Devereux, 2nd Earl of 83, 85, *86*, 92, 128, 130, 132

fatwahs 47
Ferdinand, Archduke, of Austria 17
First World War 17
Flanders 45
Flushing 43, 122, 126, 128
Franche-Comté 54, 55, 60
Frederick Henry (son of Louise de Coligny) 134
French civil wars 18, 93, 106
'French Fury' (Antwerp, 1583) 45, 93, 125, 126, 163n
Frontinus: *Stratagems* 134

Gaspar (Antwerp surgeon) 72
Gaston, Don 101
Genoa 41
Gérard, Balthasar 105, 111: birth and background 54–5; at Catholic University of Dôle 55; recruited to spy in Spanish camp 19, 50; Philip II's secret agent 19; gains access to

W 55, 108, 148; purchase of pocket pistol 56–8, 149; W's assassin 19, 20, *49, 50, 53, 54*, 113, 149–50; interrogation and torture after W's death 19, 51, 58, 150–1; confession 146–8; justification for action 111; personality 58; execution 58, 59–60
Gérard family 55, 60
Germany: evangelical Protestant princes 27
Gheeraerts, Marcus, the younger 85
'Glorious Revolution' (1688) 16
Goltzius, Hendrik 25
Granvelle, Antoine Perrenot, Cardinal: appointed Cardinal 30; Dutch nobility oppose 30; persecutes Protestants 30; erosion of nobility's secular power 30; withdrawn by Philip II 30–1, 33; and Gérard's family 55
Gravelines 133
guerrilla tactics 86
Guise, Francis, Duke of 17, *18*, 35, 106
Guise faction 36
gunpowder 78, 84
guns *see* handguns; pistols; wheel-lock pistol
Gwin, Robert 88

Habsburgs: W supported by 28; W fails to live up to their hopes 28; W seeks to distance himself from 29–30; Gérard family supports 55; Jauregay committed to 65; 'self-igniting handguns' banned 93
Hague, The 128, *129*, 133
handguns: W's murder 17, 19, 20, 26, 50; in killings of major political figures 17; three bullets in a single chamber 19, 26, 50, 150; prohibitions on 20; attempted murder of W 70; end era of the mounted knight 80–1; alter the deployment of troops in battle 84; Charles V's collection 96–7, *97*; symbolism of 112–13; proclamation

handguns – *contd.*
  against use of 155–8; *see also* pistols;
    wheel-lock pistol
Hangest, Jean de, lord of Genlis 35
Harvey, Gabriel 134
Hatton, Sir Christopher 100, 110
heavy cavalry 80–1
hedge preachers 32
Henry III, King of France 42
Herle, William 66, 118: on W's
    convalescence 72–3, 76, 162n;
    considers Elizabeth in danger
    99–101; on Zutphen 104;
    reprimanded by Leicester 105; tries
    to persuade Elizabeth to become
    involved in Dutch Revolt 122–3,
    162n; Philip II's view of English
    religion 127
highwaymen 93
Hogenburg, Frans 49, 63
Holland 141: W as stadholder 28; W
    obtains control 33–4; Dordrecht
    political assembly (1572) 37; support
    for W 42; W takes up residence 45;
    vulnerable after W's death 117
Hornes, Count of 33
House of Nassau 27
House of Orange 15, 16
House of Orange-Nassau 16
Huguenots 17, 18, 34, 35, 36
Huntingdon, Earl of 132
Hussein, Saddam 113

infantrymen 80, 81
intelligence-gatherers 18–19
Irish campaigns 86, 88, 91, 92
iron pyrites 77

James II, King of England 16, 134, 160n
Jauregay, Jean: employed by Anastro
    69, 70, 71; gains W's trust 65, 108;
    assassination attempt on W (1582)
    63, 64–5, 99, 105; death 65; papers
    found on body 67, 68; murder
    weapon 70; fate of body 71;
    justification given for action 111

Jesuits 107
John of Nassau, Count (W's brother)
    31, 36, 44
Juliana of Stolberg (W's mother) 26

Kennedy, John F. 17, 160n
Kennedy, Robert 17
King, Martin Luther 17
Knollys, Sir William 131

lances 81, 82, 83
Languet, Hubert 37, 45, 47
Laredo 69
'League of the Great' 33
Lee, Captain Thomas 85–8, 87
Lee, Sir Henry 163n
Leicester, Robert Dudley, Earl of 47,
    73, 99: and assassination attempt on
    W 67, 126; portraits of 88, 89, 90;
    and Parry 109–10; and Herle's
    verbosity 123; godfather to W's
    daughter 124; leads campaign to
    assist Dutch Protestants 88, 90–2,
    105, 127–33; accompanies Anjou to
    Low Countries 126; and Protestant
    cause 127–8; death 134
Leicester faction 102
Leiden, University of 129
Lennon, John 136
Leonardo da Vinci 78
Lepanto, Battle of (1571) 41
Leuven (Louvain), university of 33
light cavalry 80–1
light horsemen 80, 92, 131
limaçon manoeuvre 81
Lincoln, Abraham 17
Louis of Nassau, Count 34, 35
Low Countries: occupations of 15;
    political fragmentation and violent
    confrontation 18; W as defender of
    Protestant faith 28; W leads
    struggle against Habsburgs 29;
    reorganisation of bishoprics 30;
    commitment to Reformed Church
    31–2; Charles IX considers invading
    34; Alva's taxation 41; Parma

Low Countries – *contd.*
appointed Governor General (1579) 42; Anjou becomes titular ruler 42–3; Leicester's campaign to assist Dutch Protestant cause 88, 90–2, 127–33; Stanley's career in 91–2; W's death weakens position of Protestant provinces 117
Ludovick of Nassau, Count 140
Luther, Martin 32
Lyon 108

Maastricht 42
Margaret of Parma 30, 31
Marnix van St Aldegonde, Philip 47: W's secretary and confidential emissary 37; Dordrecht speech (1572) 38–9; resigns and returns home 45; inspects papers found on Jauregay's body 67; attempts to embroil Elizabeth in Dutch Revolt 123
Mary, Princess of Orange 134
Mary, Queen of Scots 17, 82, 107, 108, 109, 132
Mary II, Queen of England 16, 134
Maureval (marksman) 36
Maurice, Prince of Orange (W's son) 162n: as W's successor 33, 66; and papers found on Jauregay's body 67; and Louise de Coligny 120; stadholder and commander of Dutch armed forces 128, 134; and Leicester 128, 133
Maurice of Saxony 30
Maximilian, Emperor 93
Mechelen bishopric 30, 36, 39
Medina Sidonia, Duke of 133
Mendoza, Bernardine de 100
Meyer, A. de 162n
Mons 34–5, 36, 39
Montaigne, Michel de 93–4, 106, 163–4n
Morgan, Colonel Thomas 50, 73, 108, 109

Naarden 39–40
Nashe, Thomas: *The Unfortunate Traveller* 94–6

Nassau family 26
Netherlands: W distances himself from Habsburg cause 29–30; anti-Catholic feeling in 30; Philip II's confrontation with nobility 30; boycott of Council of State meetings 30; 'Act of Abjuration' (1581) 43
Neville, Sir Edmund 109–12, 152–4
Newgate gaol 107
Norris, Sir John: as military commander 83; skirmish engagements 84; firearms business 90; on Stanley 92; Louise de Coligny's letter 120; Elizabeth finances 123; and Leicester 130, 131, 132
North Sea 33, 128
Northern Ireland 16
Northumberland, Henry Percy, Earl of 19

Orange: death of René of Chalon 26; Habsburg possession 26; W becomes heir to Chalon estates 26; Roman remains 28–9; sovereign princes 29
Orangemen 16, 160n
Oswald, Lee Harvey 160n
Ottoman navy 40, 41

Parham House, West Sussex 90
Paris 108, 109
Parma, Duchess of 140, 144
Parma, Alexander Farnese, Duke of 44, 45, 69, 101, 130–1, 150: appointed Governor General of Low Countries (1579) 42; regains control of key towns 42, 130–1; and assassination attempt on W 51, 66; and Jauregay 70; at Zutphen 104; and fall of Antwerp 121; and Gérard 150
Parry, Dr William 106–12, 152–4
Peck, Peter 97
Pembroke, Earl of 132
Philip II, King of Spain: ruler in Low Countries 27–8, 38; W's political

Philip II, King of Spain – *contd.*
reticence 29; withdraws Granvelle
30–1; and anti-Catholic iconoclasm
32; and Calvinist worship 34; financial
problems 40–1; Battle of Lepanto 41;
W's stand against 15, 16; Proclamation
against W (the Ban; 1580) 46–7, 60–1,
120, 139–43; and W's assassination 19,
46, 47, 51, 55, 57, 60–1; and Anastro
70; and Anjou 76; possible
Anglo–French alliance against 125;
and religion of English 127
Philip of Hesse 30
Philip William, Prince of Orange (W's
eldest son) 33
pikes 81
pistoleers 81, 131
pistols 17: wheel-lock *see* wheel-lock
pistol; as fashion items 57, 58; belt-
hook 57, 88; decoration of 57, 70;
exchanged as tokens of friendship
and esteem 70–1; Leicester's
purchases 88–90; as emblem of fear
105; proclamation against 154–8; *see
also* handguns
Princeton University 16, 160n
Prinsenhof, Delft 50
Privy Council 92
Protestantism: English 105;
international cause 127–8; Sidney's
role 165n; University of Leiden 135
Protestants: antagonism towards
Catholics 18; Granvelle persecutes
30; W's attitude towards 31; and
attempts on lives of Protestant
sovereigns 112
Pynoie, Princess of 66

Al Qaida 114
Quinborough (Queenborough)
Castle, Kent 152

Reformed Church 31–2
reiters (riders) 81, 83, 88
René of Chalon (W's uncle) 26, 139
Rheims 108

Rizzio, David 17
Rome 108
Rotterdam 122
Rubens, Jan 160n
Rubens, Peter Paul 160n
Ruby, Jack 160n

St Bartholomew's Day Massacre (1572)
18, 36, 45, 93
St Ghislain 35
Sarajevo 17
Scaevola, Mucius 88, 163n
Schoonhoven negotiations 31
Shakur, Tupac 136
Sidney, Sir Philip: favourite of Queen
Elizabeth 81; as *reiter* 81; attends
W's daughter's christening 124;
influence on Anglo–Dutch
Protestant affairs 124; accompanies
Anjou to Low Countries 126; as
Leicester's guide and facilitator 128;
fatally wounded at Zutphen 81, 83,
91, 105, 131–2
Sidney, Sir Robert 131
Somerville (Somerfield), John 105–6, 111
Spain: threatens to strengthen hold
on Dutch coastline 20; and W's
domination of coastline 33–4;
Inquisition 34
Spanish Armada (1588) 16, 117, 133–4
Spanish army: and W's volunteer
forces 33; 'Spanish Fury' at Antwerp
41; consolidation 130–1
Spanish Netherlands 91
Stafford, Sir Edward 102
Stanley, Sir William 91–2
Sussex, Earl of 100

Tate Britain Gallery, London 85
Temmerman, Antonin 71, 162n
Tower of London 19, 110

Unton, Sir Henry 131
Utrecht 28, 37

Vatican 36

Venero, Antonio de 69, 70, 71
Venice 93
Victoria and Albert Museum, London 97
Villiers, Pierre Loyseleur de 37, 55–6, 57, 67, 126
Votallys (doctor) 72
Vuillafans, Franche-Comté, France 54, 161n

Walsingham, Sir Francis 76, 83, 91, 100, 102, 123: supports W 47; reports on W's assassination 51–2; and assassination attempt on W 73; and Somerville 106; negotiates with States General 124; and international Protestant cause 127–8; uncovers Babington Plot 132
Webster, John: *The White Devil* 94
Westminster, London 110
wheel-lock pistol 17, 20, 57–8, 61, 77–98, 131, 136, 162n: on the battlefield 77–84; mechanism *78*, 78–80; gun culture 85–92; symbolism 90–1; used in self-defence 93–5; élite toy and fashionable accessory 96–8
Whitehall Palace, London 108
William III, King of England 16, 134, 160n
William, Prince of Orange, Count of Nassau ('William the Silent') 25: family tree 22–3; birth 26; upbringing 26, 27; elevation of 26–7; stand against Philip II 15, 16; reason for nickname 16, 27, 29; personality 27; at Charles V's court 26, 27; attitude to religion 27, 31; enters Council of State 27; Knight of the Order of the Golden Fleece 28; Charles V's trust 28; stadholder of Holland, Zeeland and Utrecht 28, 32; marriages 29–30, 45, 74, 124,

160n; Schoonhoven negotiations 31; pressured by Philip to impose direct Spanish rule 32; withdraws to German Nassau territories 32; Dutch properties and revenues confiscated 32–3; forces driven back by Alva 33; invades Brabant 36; creates base for Orangist forces 37; creation of image as hero 37, 39; and Duke of Anjou 42, 43–4, 45; assassination attempt on (1582) 20, 44, 61, 64–7, 99, 104, 105; recovery 72–6; takes up residence in Delft 45; proscription against (1580) 46–7, 60–1, 120, 144–5; negotiations for title of 'Count of Holland and Zeeland' 46, 48; publication of 'Apology' 47, 120; anomalous position 48, 61; hopes for a moderate, intellectual Protestantism 129; assassination (1584) 17, 19, 20, 26, 49, 50, 51, 52, *54*, 99, 102; 'deathbed utterances' 52; burial 151; significance of murder 16–17, 19–20, 53, 58, 88, 132, 136, *see also* English aftermath to W's murder
William the Rich (W's father) 26
Williams, Sir Roger 50, 51, 83, 131, 149: *Briefe Discourse of War* 83
Willoughby, Peregrine, Lord 131

Yzunça, Jean de 69–70

Zeeland 122, 141: W as stadholder 28; W obtains control 33–4; Dordrecht political assembly (1572) 37; supports W 42; vulnerable after W's death 117
Zutphen: sacked by Alba (1572) 39; strategic importance 104; Leicester's loss of control of 105
Zutphen, Battle of (1586) 83, 91–2, 105, 131–2